Contents

BABY'S FIRST YEAR

A Parent's Guide

**Shanta
Everington**

Baby's First Year – A Parent's Guide is also available in accessible formats for people with any degree of visual impairment. The large print edition and eBook (with accessibility features enabled) are available from Need2Know. Please let us know if there are any special features you require and we will do our best to accommodate your needs.

First published in Great Britain in 2011 by
Need2Know
Remus House
Coltsfoot Drive
Peterborough
PE2 9BF
Telephone 01733 898103
Fax 01733 313524
www.need2knowbooks.co.uk

Introduction

Welcoming your new baby into the world is one of the most amazing experiences you are ever likely to encounter. It can also be one of the most daunting, as you are faced with this tiny, fragile, new person who is entirely dependent on you for their every need. Gulp!

Nobody is born knowing how to be a parent. The truth is that nobody can tell you how to be a good parent, because there is no single right way to do things. But it does help to be prepared and informed about babies' needs and key stages of development.

This book is written by a parent who understands the excitement and fear you are likely to be feeling right now. Combining my own personal experience and a wide range of family case studies, with underpinning parenting theory and practical strategies, this guide will provide you with information and support to help you find your feet during baby's first year.

You may find yourself asking questions like these:

- Why is my new baby crying all the time?
- How can I help prevent nappy rash?
- Should I breastfeed or bottle feed?
- What is the best way to put my baby to bed?
- When will my baby start sleeping through the night?
- How can I soothe my baby during teething?
- When and how should I start weaning my baby on to solids?
- When can I expect my baby to start crawling?

These are all questions that will be addressed in this book. New babies don't come with instructions, but that doesn't mean that there aren't plenty of baby manuals out there to tell you what you should be doing. When my son was born, I read everything about babies that I could get my hands on.

'Parenting is unique and individual to each family. Each family must find out what suits them and their lifestyle choices - not a prescriptive template from which we all have to follow. Of course, it is nice to get ideas from others.'

Avvai, mum to two children (aged one and four).

I was armed with feeding schedules, sleep techniques, contented baby routines, medical facts, psychobabble ideas and social essays. Whatever question about babies I needed answering, there were a hundred conflicting opinions to be read, digested and applied. It was enough to drive the sanest person mad with confusion.

Many baby manuals will present you with prescriptive advice as though there is only one way to do things. Only you can decide what sort of parent you want to be – there are many different approaches to parenting and some will fit in with your values and lifestyle, and others will not.

However, by reading this book you will learn:

- How to adjust to new parenthood and look after yourself and your baby.
- How to bond and interact with your baby and offer stimulating activities.
- Ways to establish successful feeding and deal with possible problems.
- To understand the main causes of baby's crying and how to respond.
- How to help your baby settle down to sleep at night.
- Strategies for soothing a teething baby.
- To understand the key stages of your baby's physical development.
- Some tips for starting your child on to solids at an appropriate time.
- How to avoid burnout as a new parent and when to seek help.

This essential guide will provide practical strategies to guide you step by step through your baby's first year. Nobody can ever know your baby like you. While you get to know your baby's needs, this book aims to arm you with essential knowledge and resources to help make your first year of parenthood as stress-free and enjoyable as possible.

Whether you are reading the book while pregnant or have already had your baby, I hope this guide will help you to find your feet, trust your instincts and enjoy your new baby.

'I wasn't at all prepared for the strength of the love I'd feel for my daughter . . . the absolute and unconditional love. It really is an amazing feeling and puts everything into perspective. When Aimee smiles at me or looks for me, it just reminds me how much I love being Aimee's mum.'

Caroline, mum to Aimee (aged four months).

Acknowledgements

This book is dedicated to my son, Etienne (aka Smallboy), who taught me how to be a parent; to my mum and dad, who are the best parents one could ask for; and to my husband, Raymond, for sharing the journey.

I am grateful to the many people who helped me throughout the writing and publication of this guide. First, I must thank Trudi Maples and Eve Hopping at Need2Know Books for bringing the book out. Enormous thanks to all the amazing parents who so generously shared their experiences with me in person and online. It was a privilege to hear your stories. To Avvai, Agnes, Caroline Murray, Dawn, Fiona, Josephine, Pauline, Rachel Pattisson and Vusi Coe, thank you for allowing me to quote you in the guide. (Some parents have been acknowledged by first name only and others quoted by pseudonym, as requested to protect privacy.)

Disclaimer

This book is primarily a collection of ideas and is not intended as a substitute for individual professional advice. The author advises that she does not claim medical qualifications. Anyone with concerns about parental or baby's physical or emotional wellbeing should consult their doctor or health visitor for individual advice.

'It wasn't until the baby was about a year old that I realised that there is no magic bullet.'

Pauline, mum to two children (aged one and three).

Chapter One

The First Few Weeks

'I laugh with tears streaming down my face at this creature who has ripped my body apart and turned it inside out. It is truly a miracle, and I realise at this precise moment that I've just discovered the secrets of the universe and at the same time, know absolutely nothing at all.' Extract from the author's journal, written in the first year of motherhood.

Adjusting to parenthood

No matter how prepared you think you are for becoming a parent, it's likely that the first few weeks will come as something of a shock for new mums and dads alike! So, if despite your joy and love for your new baby, you aren't in a perpetual state of bliss, fear not. You are normal.

Adjusting to parenthood is a major life transition and one that can take time. Some people seem to take to parenthood like a duck to water, whereas others might find it takes a little longer to settle into. Remember that lots of new parents hide their anxieties in public. You know that new mum or dad you've seen, the one who looks so utterly calm and under control with their lovely new buggy and matching changing bag? They probably don't look like that behind closed doors. Not all the time anyway. We all have our moments.

When embarking on a new career, you don't expect yourself to learn everything in the first five minutes, and parenthood is no different. You may have heard the saying that parenthood is a 24-hour job with no holidays! It's not all doom and gloom; it has a lot of perks too. But just as you would need to pace yourself if you were starting a training course, it's important to pace yourself in those early days and weeks of parenthood too. You are learning on the job and there are only three certainties involved:

- You will make mistakes.
- You will get exhausted.
- You will learn.

Baby blues

It is very common for new mums to experience what is termed 'the baby blues'. This can involve feeling down and tearful soon after the birth. This is partly to do with hormonal changes in the body, a bit like when you get PMT, and also to do with the huge emotional shock of having a tiny baby dependent on you.

Postnatal depression

The medical establishment differentiates between baby blues, which is very common, and postnatal depression (PND), which is said to affect one in 10 women. The term 'postnatal depression' is a medical label that some women may not feel comfortable identifying with. But the important thing is to feel able to seek support when needed. Your doctor or health visitor can be a good starting point.

It used to be believed that PND was caused solely by hormonal imbalance. However, more recently, it has been recognised that social factors can also contribute to new mothers becoming depressed. The lack of a supportive partner or family or friends close by, and problems with housing, finances or employment can all be factors. (Clinical Knowledge Summaries, 2009.) For more information on PND, take a look at *Postnatal Depression – The Essential Guide* (Catherine Burrows, Need2Know).

Fathers have feelings too

Remember that new dads can also struggle in the early days and feel overwhelmed by the responsibility of new parenthood. It may be more difficult for a father to admit to these feelings, as he may feel that he needs to be 'strong' for the mother. For more support for the new dad, take a look at *Fatherhood – The Essential Guide* (Tim Atkinson, Need2Know).

'I cried every day for the first few weeks, possibly months. I was at home, alone, with a young baby who I thought might possibly have something wrong with her (she didn't). I felt desperately sad that I wasn't loving every moment of being a parent.'

Pauline, mum to two children (aged one and three).

New parent's mantra

It's important for both new mums and dads to cut themselves a bit of slack and seek support when needed. We will talk more about this in the final chapter.

And when things do get difficult, hold on to the parent's mantra:

This too will pass.

What you'll need

What do you need to look after your new baby? The truth lies somewhere between two extremes. On the one hand, newborns require very little. A few Babygros, a pack of nappies and somewhere comfy to sleep is really all that is required.

On the other hand, as we all know, along with the baby seems to come an enormous amount of paraphernalia: the cot, pram, baby carrier, bath, feeding cushion, nursing bra, steriliser, breast pump, breast pads, changing bag, going home outfit, mobile, baby gym, bouncy chair, baby swing . . .

Some parents like to get everything ready in advance, whereas others start with the basics and acquire what they need as they go on. If you have friends or family with children, you may be able to borrow some baby care items from seasoned parents whose children are no longer babies. If you are given a Moses basket, crib or cot, you should buy a new mattress for your baby for safety reasons.

The checklist overleaf can be a useful starting point for working out what you've got and what you may need in the early days. Further details can be found in relevant chapters e.g. chapter 2 – Feeding Options, chapter 4 – Sleep, chapter 5 – Keeping Baby Clean.

'I had very little experience of babies, hadn't even so much as changed a nappy before. People assumed because I was older and sort of "middle class" I knew what I was doing. I didn't. It does get easier though for any parents out there feeling the same.'

Josephine (mum to Tom, aged 10 months).

Baby care equipment checklist

Sleeping	Feeding	Bathing	Changing	Clothes	Carrying
Moses basket, carry cot, crib or cot	Breast-feeding:	Baby bath or bath aid to use in main bath	Disposable nappies or re-usable nappies	Babygros – short-sleeved & long-sleeved	Sling/ baby carrier
Mattress	Nursing bras	Baby sponge	Changing mat	Separates (tops and bottoms)	Pram or buggy
Sheets & blankets	Breast pads	Soft towel	Cotton wool	Jumpers/ cardigans for colder weather	Infant car seat
Cot mobile	Breast pump		Baby lotion/ oil	Hats, socks and mittens	NB some travel systems combine car seat with buggy
Baby monitor	Bottle feeding:			Bibs	
	Bottles with newborn-size teats				
	Steriliser				
	Infant formula				

'Eventually, I bought a sling so that the baby could be close to me all the time (something people told me was variously: getting the baby into bad habits; would encourage it to sleep; would mean that it wouldn't want to be put down to sleep on its own etc) and I went out a lot!'

Pauline, mum to two children (aged one and three).

Your newborn

When you meet your new baby for the first time, you may feel scared that you don't know how to hold them or what to do with them! This is a natural fear but will quickly subside as you get used to handling your newborn.

Interesting fact

According to Dr. Miriam Stoppard in New Baby Care, the average birth weight is 5lb 8oz to 9lb 12oz and the average length of a newborn is 19 to 20 inches.

Need2Know

When your baby is born, they have to adjust to being outside of your body for the first time. Every sensation is new for them and it takes them time to get used to the change. It makes sense then that many babies like to be held and carried around. Babies like to hear their mother's heartbeat, just as they did when they were inside their mother's body.

While in the womb, your baby got used to your daily movements. They didn't spend nine months lying flat and motionless and therefore, probably won't particularly welcome this afterwards!

Baby wearing

One way to help your baby adjust to life outside the body is by using a sling or baby carrier to keep your baby close to you. Some people refer to this as 'baby wearing'. There are lots of different types and models of slings and baby carriers on the market that you can try out.

Skin-to-skin

Like other mammals, human babies are designed to respond to touch and like to be held. New babies enjoy lots of direct skin-to-skin contact. Allow your baby to lie against your bare chest wearing just their nappy. Skin-to-skin contact between mother and baby has been shown to help with breastfeeding. Dads can also take part in skin-to-skin contact with their new babies.

Head control

When you pick your newborn up and put them down, it is important to support their head, so that it doesn't flop back, as new babies have little head control. By the time your baby is about a month old, they are likely to be able to control their head better. It's generally advisable to pick your newborn up gently and slowly at first until they get stronger and more used to being handled.

'I think we can learn a lot from other mammals and how they treat their young offspring – always keeping them close and being fiercely protective of them and then when they feel they have taught them what they can, they let them go . . . '

Avvai, mum to two children (aged one and four).

Getting to know your baby

Although your baby is part of you and has been growing inside you for nine months, you still need to get to know them as you would with any new person that you meet. Although some behaviour is common to all newborns, all babies are individuals with different ways, likes, dislikes and needs. The best way to get to know your baby is by observing them closely.

Newborn behaviour

It is common for newborns to make snuffling noises when they breathe, to sneeze and hiccup quite a lot. This is nothing to worry about. Of course, if you ever sense that your baby is having difficulty breathing, this would be a different matter and cause for medical attention.

Reflexes

Babies, like other mammals, are born with automatic reflexes, which have developed to ensure survival of the human species. The resulting movements are involuntary. Reflexes include:

- The rooting reflex – when the baby roots for the breast to feed.
- The sucking reflex – all babies have a powerful desire to suck.
- The swallowing reflex – babies can swallow from birth.
- The grasp reflex – newborns will powerfully grip an object placed in their hands.
- The startle reflex, also known as the Moro reflex – babies respond to loud noises and rough handling.

'Baby-led parenting is about taking cues from the baby and responding to them; each baby is different and has different needs. One size doesn't fit all and it's about mother and baby developing their own dance and being in tune with each other.'

Avvai, mum to two children (aged one and four).

Parent–baby bonding

Your newborn baby will probably spend most of their time sleeping during the early days (although it might not always feel like it, especially if you have a colicky baby!). It is important to spend the little time that they are awake bonding with them.

Babies respond to touch, smell and sound, and will use their senses to recognise and bond with their mummy and daddy. Your baby will get to know the sound of your voice, your unique smell and touch. The importance of physical contact must not be underestimated.

Why I wrote this guide

During my pregnancy, I hadn't really thought about what was coming next. Of course, I thought about the birth. The antenatal classes made sure of that. But I didn't spend too many moments thinking about what it would actually mean to be responsible for a brand new, tiny little speck of a person who was dependent on me for his every need. It sounds ridiculous, but many parents have said the same.

As a first timer, I was desperate to know how I could possibly morph into this mysterious magical being of 'parent'. When the baby slept (which didn't seem very often) I read everything I could find on the subject of babies. I read. And I read. And I tried to find the answers.

The problem was that my baby didn't do what it said in the manuals. He slept when he should be awake and screamed when he should be asleep. He squirmed at the breast and refused the bottle. He cried when I picked him up and cried when I put him down. Clearly one of us wasn't working properly.

One sunny afternoon, after listening to me complaining about how confused and stressed and tired I was, my older sister gathered all the tear-stained, milk-smeared how-to books up off the floor, stuffed them in her rucksack and left me with her parting words, 'These books are only making you feel worse. Just do what you feel works for you.' She was right. I knew she was right. But the problem was I had no idea what might work for me.

That evening, the baby cried. I picked him up. He cried. I offered him milk. He cried. I checked his nappy. He cried. I put him down. He cried. I walked him around the room. We both cried. I wanted a no-nonsense, fifties maternity nurse in a starchy apron to tell me what to do. But Gina Ford and Supernanny were gone. I slung the baby over my shoulder and opened one of the books my sister hadn't confiscated. A social perspective on motherhood. How was I supposed to get to grips with social theory when I hadn't slept for two weeks and I barely had time to read the TV magazine? And how was it going to actually help me?

What I really wanted was a book written by someone who understood. I wanted to read about other parents' experiences. I wanted somebody to tell me it was going to be okay. *Baby's First Year: A Parent's Guide* is the book I craved when I came home from hospital as a woman with a baby and struggled to become a parent. If you are a new parent, I hope it will help you trust yourself and find your own way.

Summing Up

Becoming a parent for the first time is a joyous and exciting time, but can also be a time of anxiety. It takes time to adjust to the responsibilities of new parenthood.

Baby's first year is a time of huge learning and development for both new parents and baby alike. Your baby is experiencing everything for the first time and learning new skills every day. You are learning what it means to be a parent and what approach works best for your family.

Like everything in life, developing parenting skills takes practice, patience and trial and error. There are no magic answers, but trusting your instincts and sharing ideas and experiences can go a long way towards helping you feel able to handle all life has to throw at you as a new mum or dad!

Chapter Two

Feeding Options

'Like all Good Mummies, I was going to breastfeed. I'd listened carefully during my antenatal class. I'd studied the diagrams in the manuals. It was hardly rocket science, was it? Millions of women did it every day. It never once entered my head that things might actually go wrong!' Extract from the author's journal, written in the first year of motherhood.

Breast or bottle?

Breastfeeding

Department of Health guidelines recommend exclusive breastfeeding for the first six months. Not many people will contest that 'breast is best'. After all, it is the only food that is specifically designed to meet your baby's needs. Packed full of nutrients, breastmilk also contains antibodies that help build up your baby's immune system.

Once established, many women find breastfeeding easier on a practical level too. You don't need to spend any time making a bottle, counting scoops of formula milk, warming the bottle at the right temperature, washing or sterilising bottles. With breastfeeding, the milk is always ready and at the right temperature and you can feed any time of day or night, any place. It also helps you to lose your pregnancy weight.

However, in England, statistics from the second quarter of 2010/11 showed that the prevalence of breastfeeding at 6-8 weeks was only 46.2% of babies due a 6-8 week check. (*Source: Statistical release: breastfeeding initiation and prevalence at 6-8 weeks, www.dh.gov.uk*) So why are less than half of new mums managing to breastfeed?

'Feeding on demand meant that in the first few months, it didn't feel like I had a lot of time left to do anything else! I felt that feeding my son was my most important role as his mother, so I didn't mind. I enjoyed it most of the time and considered it as a privilege and bonding moment with my baby.'

Agnes, mum to Edgar (aged 10 months).

Breastfeeding does not always 'come naturally'. Like anything new, it can take time and practice to establish. However, with a hungry newborn to feed, new mums don't always feel that they have the luxury of time to get it right, and without the right support in those critical early days, breastfeeding can fall at the first hurdle.

It can be helpful to know in advance what some of the potential problems might be and how to resolve them, as well as how to seek support should this be needed. And if things don't work out with breastfeeding, it is important to be able to feel okay about this.

Bottle feeding

Some women may choose not to breastfeed at all, opting for the bottle from the outset. It is not a crime. Others may want to breastfeed but find it doesn't work for them, for a variety of reasons. When celebrity mother, Denise van Outen, stopped breastfeeding after three weeks, there was a national outcry!

Sadly, society can be very harsh and judgmental towards mothers. Society tells us that 'breast is best' yet breastfeeding in public can still be frowned upon. Sometimes it seems that new mothers can do no right.

Every woman's decision about how to feed her baby is personal to her and no mother should be judged because of this. Bottle-fed babies do perfectly well and it is a myth that bonding with your baby will suffer if you do not breastfeed. You can still have plenty of cuddles and skin-to-skin contact regardless.

This chapter aims to equip you with plenty of useful information and tips to make your feeding experiences happy and successful, whatever you decide.

> **'DVDs that said breastfeeding should be "completely comfortable if done properly" did not seem particularly helpful to me. I wish that the information provided upfront had been more honest.'**
>
> Dawn, mum to Leila (aged 10 months).

Interesting fact

A newborn baby's stomach is only about the size of a marble, so they have to feed little and often in the early days.

Establishing breastfeeding

If you do decide to breastfeed, it is generally advised to put your baby to your breast as soon as they are born. Their natural rooting reflex will mean that they search for the nipple and may feed straight away. Skin-to-skin contact is also thought to encourage breastfeeding.

Interesting fact

Your breasts initially produce a substance called colostrum which contains lots of antibodies to help protect your baby. After two or three days, the milk will start to be produced.

If breastfeeding doesn't come naturally straight away, don't despair. Many women experience difficulties at the start. After all, this is something you've never done before and both you and your baby are getting to grips with the skills involved.

Case study

Dawn is mum to Leila, aged 10 months, and has breastfed on demand since day one. Leila and Dawn took to breastfeeding well, although Dawn's nipples were very painful for the first few weeks. Dawn talked to the breastfeeding advisor at the hospital and the community midwife about how painful it was and they both told her that Leila wasn't latching on properly. However, when Dawn showed them what they were doing, they said it was fine.

When Leila was a newborn, she was taking around nine feeds per day. Dawn continues to breastfeed Leila at 10 months, alongside giving her daughter solids. Most days now, they do five feeds: when it starts to get light, about 7.30-8.00 am, between meals and last thing at night. If things have been disrupted for any reason, they sometimes do more feeds, but they're often very short. Dawn is preparing to stop the daytime feeds soon as she will be returning to work when Leila is one.

'Don't be scared to ask for help. It can take a while before you feel confident breastfeeding. Your midwife or health visitor can support you.'

NHS breastfeeding website.

Latching on

Your baby is born with a natural rooting reflex and will root for your nipple if you put them to the breast. If you stroke your baby's cheek nearest the breast, they will turn towards your breast. However, they might need a bit of encouragement to actually latch on to your breast sufficiently to feed.

In order for your baby to latch on to your breast, it is important to try to get as much of the areola (the area around the nipple) in as possible. This is because pressure needs to be exerted on the milk ducts behind the areola for your milk to be expressed. If your nipple is not far enough inside your baby's mouth, your milk may not come out properly and your nipple is more likely to get sore.

Let down reflex

When your baby sucks at your breast, hormones are released which stimulate your milk glands to produce milk and pass it to the milk reservoirs behind the areola. This is known as the 'let down reflex'. Some women feel their breasts produce milk at the sight or sound of their babies, even before they have put them to the breast.

If your let down reflex is very strong and your milk is pouring out very quickly, you might find it helpful to express a little milk before your baby latches on in the early days.

How long and how often to feed

In the early days, feeding little and often is a good idea. A baby will generally take about 80% of the feed in the first five minutes. Newborns may need to be fed every two hours. By one month, this may move to every three hours and by three months every four hours.

However, these are just averages. All babies have different feeding needs so it is a good idea to be led by your baby. When they appear to have had enough of one breast, try the other. If they are not interested, start with the other breast next time.

'I soon realised that milk comes and goes. Some days you have lots, others you have less, but if you carry on feeding, there's always going to be more milk. Some days, I felt like I didn't have much milk, but Edgar was always able to make it arrive just by sucking.'

Agnes, mum to Edgar (aged 10 months.)

If you allow your baby to feed on demand, they will usually let you know when they have had enough by losing interest in feeding or by falling asleep. It is believed to be impossible to overfeed a breastfed baby, as they will take what they need. However, be aware that your baby may continue sucking for comfort even when they are no longer hungry.

How to remove your baby from the breast

Make sure your baby's mouth is open before you attempt to remove them from the breast. You can do this by pressing their chin down or putting your little finger in the corner of their mouth.

Positions for breastfeeding

There are many different possible positions for breastfeeding. You can breastfeed sitting up with your baby on your lap or lying down with your baby alongside you. It is a good idea to vary your position throughout the day as this will help minimise the risk of blocked milk ducts.

Pillows and cushions

Pillows and cushions can be useful for support. There are a range of specially designed pillows on the market that are intended for breastfeeding use, such as wedge-shaped cushions and V-shaped pillows. These are designed to be used on your lap, while you are sitting. You then place the baby on the cushion to raise them to the correct height.

Expressing milk

Many mums choose to express milk. This can then be stored in the fridge or freezer and given to your baby later. The advantage of doing this is the baby's dad or someone else can bottle feed the baby.

'I would express a bottle a day so that her dad could be involved in feeding. If her granny was babysitting I'd try to express a couple of bottles to be safe. At first I felt really uncomfortable with other people feeding Leila.'

Dawn, mum to Leila (aged 10 months).

Breast pumps

Some mums choose to express by hand, but there are also a range of pumps available on the market to help speed things up if required! These include manually operated pumps, as well as electrical ones. A suction cup fits over your breast and when you operate the pump, your milk will be expressed into the attached container. You can even get pumps with dual cups that enable you to express from both breasts at the same time.

Buying a brand new electrical breast pump can be expensive so it is worth being aware that it is possible to hire breast pumps for a fixed period of time, which involves less financial outlay. The NCT (National Childbirth Trust) offers this service.

Interesting fact

The Equality Act, which came into law in England and Wales in October 2010, makes it clear that it is sex discrimination to treat a woman unfavourably because she is breastfeeding. This means that it is illegal for a shop, bus driver or benefits office to ask a woman to stop breastfeeding or leave. Similar protection applies in Scotland and Northern Ireland.

Possible feeding problems and remedies

Flat or inverted nipples

Some new mums experience problems with latching on because their nipples do not protrude enough. In most cases, a nipple shield can help.

Case study

At first, Agnes found that her baby Edgar couldn't latch on properly as her nipple didn't protrude enough. She kept trying but it wasn't working and Edgar was getting increasingly frustrated with every attempt. With the hours passing and him not feeding, the midwives started to pressure Agnes into giving her son a bottle. However, Agnes really wanted to breastfeed and feared that giving him a bottle might mean he would never accept the breast, so she stood her ground.

At the same time, Agnes was worried and didn't know whether she should follow the midwives' advice or her own instinct. Agnes says it was very stressful and unsettling, as she was also receiving contradictory information from the midwives. In the end, about 24 hours after he was born, one of the midwives suggested that Agnes try using a nipple shield. It was amazing. Within two seconds, Edgar was latched on and feeding as if it was the most natural thing!

Agnes and Edgar used the nipple shield for about three months, after which time Agnes gradually weaned him off the shield and continued to breastfeed until he was 10 months old.

Cracked nipples

Cracked nipples can be very painful. To help prevent cracked nipples, feed little and often in the first few days to give your nipples a chance to harden. Breast pads can help to keep the nipples dry. Some mothers may find nipple cream helps. If you do experience a cracked nipple, it is advised to express milk by hand from the affected breast and not feed from that breast until it heals.

Engorged/swollen breasts

It is important to feed your baby often to help prevent your breasts from becoming engorged. Expressing milk can also help.

Blocked milk ducts

Milk ducts can sometimes become blocked, often as a result of engorgement. Frequent feeding and expressing can help. Changing feeding positions during the day also helps.

Cluster feeding

Cluster feeding refers to a situation where your baby wants to have a lot of feeds very close together for a period of time. Feeding patterns do change and this doesn't usually last very long.

Breastfeeding strikes

Conversely, your baby may appear to go 'on strike' from breastfeeding for a short while and then quite happily start again.

Getting support

Friends or family who have breastfed may be able to offer useful tips. A midwife or health visitor can also offer advice, although bear in mind that they might not be mothers themselves. Many new mothers find a breastfeeding counsellor invaluable. A breastfeeding counsellor will be a mother who breastfed her own child and who has completed relevant training. For details on how to find a breastfeeding counsellor, see the help list.

Bottle feeding

There is a lot of pressure to breastfeed and if things don't work out or you have simply chosen to bottle feed, you may experience feelings of loss or guilt. Talking things through can be helpful in overcoming these feelings and moving on. Your baby will be fine if bottle fed.

'From about eight to 10 weeks, Leila would feed for hours at a stretch in the evenings with only a couple of 10-minute breaks. Nobody had told me about cluster feeding. Fortunately it was only two weeks and I got to watch a lot of TV! At the time it was quite depressing though, as I basically felt like a cow!'

Dawn, mum to Leila (aged 10 months).

It is not generally considered politically correct to espouse the joys of bottle feeding but let's face it, there are some advantages, including being able to share the night feeds with Daddy! (Of course, dads can also get involved by feeding baby a bottle of expressed breast milk, not just formula.)

Equipment

If you are bottle feeding, you will need the following items of equipment:

- Bottles with newborn-size teats – it is important to get the right teat for the age of your baby as older stage teats allow greater milk flow.
- Steriliser – for sterilising bottles and other equipment.
- Infant formula – there are many brands on the market to choose from.

You may also find the following items useful:

- A milk powder dispenser – to enable you to dispense a pre-measured amount of milk when you are out and about.
- A bottle warmer – this is handy to warm up bottles in the night. You can also get travel bottle warmers, for when you are out and about.

Making up bottles

Infant formula is basically powdered cows' milk with added nutrients. You need to make up the milk using cooled boiled water. You can also buy ready-made liquid cartons, which are handy for out and about, but more expensive.

Always wash your hands before making up the bottle and ensure that all equipment is sterilised. It is important that you make up the bottle by following the instructions and you do not over or under dilute the formula, which could make your baby ill.

Always test the temperature on your wrist before offering to your baby. If your baby doesn't drink all of the bottle, you still need to throw it away and offer a fresh one at the next feed as germs will breed.

'At around eight and a half months Leila went on a breastfeeding strike for 48 hours. I thought she'd taken a unilateral decision to give up the boob, and I was surprised by how upsetting I found it.'

Dawn, mum to Leila (aged 10 months).

How much to feed

As with breastfed babies, bottle-fed babies will differ in their feeding needs. However, bottle-fed babies tend to feed less often and will usually feed every three to four hours. The formula packet will tell you the amount of formula to offer according to age. Never force your baby to finish the feed if they don't want it. You can still feed on demand if you are using the bottle, by paying attention to your baby's behaviour and cries.

Winding

Wind your baby after feeding by gently rubbing their back. This is to help them burp and bring up any air that they have swallowed during feeding, which tends to happen more regularly in bottle-fed babies.

Combining breast and bottle feeding

At first, it is generally advised not to try to combine the two methods as your baby will get confused and it can also affect your milk supply. If you are breastfeeding, it may be possible to introduce supplementary bottles once breastfeeding is well established. Talk to your health visitor or breastfeeding counsellor about your plans.

If you have no plans to breastfeed and want to bottle feed from the outset, it is still a good idea to put the baby to the breast in the first few days so that they can benefit from the antibodies in your colostrum.

Summing Up

It can take time to establish breastfeeding, so don't panic if it doesn't seem to come naturally at first. Successful breastfeeding takes time and practice and it is important to seek help if needed.

There is a lot of pressure to breastfeed and if you choose to bottle feed, for whatever reason, you may experience difficult feelings and reactions. Again, seek support if needed.

Remember that however you choose to feed your baby, they will be fine.

Chapter Three

Crying

'"He's been crying all morning," I sighed, suddenly feeling faint and remembering that I hadn't eaten breakfast. "I need him to stay asleep long enough for me to eat a sandwich."' Extract from the author's journal, written in the first year of motherhood.

All babies cry. Some babies cry a lot. While some babies seem naturally placid and content to lie back staring at their cot mobiles and cooing for hours, others seem to scream every waking moment and need to be held a lot. Nobody really knows why some babies cry more than others, but just as all adults are different in temperament, so are little people.

If you have the latter variety, as I did, there may be days when you wonder what on earth you are supposed to do to soothe your angry, howling child. There may be days when you wonder whether you actually have the skills for the job, whether you were cut out to be a parent at all. These feelings are all perfectly natural, so don't feel bad or ashamed if you have days like this.

Why babies cry

Initially, crying is the only way that babies can communicate to let you know that they are hungry, cold, uncomfortable, lonely or just plain grouchy. As you get to know your baby, you will gradually learn how to identify what their cries mean.

After your baby is born, they have to get used to a completely new environment after being tucked away in the womb for nine months. There are lots of new sensations, such as noises and lights, and discomforts such as hunger, for them to cope with.

'A few weeks ago I met up with a friend whose baby is a couple of months younger than mine. He's always been an "angel" baby, but he was very unsettled and crying a lot, as he was teething. She was doing her best to settle him, but at one point said to me, "I just don't know what to do. He won't stop crying."'

Josephine, mum to Tom (aged 10 months).

There can be times when your baby appears to be crying for no apparent reason. They have been changed, fed, winded and cuddled and they are still crying! Some babies just don't seem to like being babies very much and need a lot of comfort.

This doesn't necessarily mean that they will grow up to be 'spoilt' or 'difficult'. There is no reason to believe that a baby who seems to cry a lot more than the average will grow up to be an unhappy child. Babyhood is a particular stage and all babies cope differently with it.

Good babies

I hate the question, 'Is she a good baby?' because there is no such thing as a 'good' or 'bad' baby. Babies are just babies! It's just that some babies may be 'easier to manage' than others.

It is worth noting that being easy or difficult to manage depends on the temperament of the parent as much as the baby. Some parents are more laid back about crying, whereas others find it more stressful. If you are naturally a perfectionist in other areas of your life, you may be likely to be the type of parent that worries about everything, especially with your first baby.

What is colic?

Many babies experience uncontrollable crying for the first three months or so, which is often put down to colic. So what exactly is colic and how can you avoid or treat it? The truth is that even the so-called 'experts' cannot agree on exactly what colic is or what causes it . . .

Some say that colic is like indigestion and appears to be worse in bottle-fed babies. Others propose that something went wrong with evolution and human babies aren't in fact ready to be born until twelve months, which is why they cry for the first three months. Another suggestion is that colic is just a word made up to describe excessive, unexplained crying. Popular opinion is that it all gets better after three months.

Colic remedies

Despite the lack of clarity on the nature and cause of colic, remedies in the form of 'colic drops' are available from chemists. These are designed to treat colic as a digestive complaint, so the success will vary depending on the cause of the baby's crying and distress.

Recognising your baby's needs

All babies are different so what works for one baby might not work for another. While your friend's baby may love being out and about all day and sleep anywhere he is put down for a nap, yours may get irritable and upset and only seem to settle in their own cot.

Getting to know your own baby's unique personality, ways and needs is much more important than pursuing endless activities or blindly following prescriptive schedules because it is what everyone else is doing.

'I've learnt what will comfort my son and what his personality is. For example, I can't really do more than one big activity, such as swimming, per day as he gets too over-tired and over-stimulated and ends up just screaming.'

Josephine (mum to Tom, aged 10 months).

Case study

Josephine's son, Tom, started screaming around four in the afternoon and would continue till about seven, just before her husband got home from work. At one point she got so low that she started to feel like the baby hated her, he seemed so angry. She questioned whether she was really up to the task of being a mother.

'It was three months of sheer hell,' says Josephine. 'Then it suddenly stops and it's like you've got a different baby. Whether it's unconditional love for your child, or what I don't know, but somehow you find the resources within yourself to manage.'

Josephine says she loves being a mum now. 'I've always loved my son but I do enjoy being with him now. As they get older they start to interact with you more and you start to understand them, their personality and their needs, so it does get easier, much easier.'

Responding to your baby's cry

The first step is to consider why your baby might be crying and to address that need. For instance, is your baby:

- Hungry or thirsty?
- Tired or over-stimulated?
- Wet or dirty?
- Lonely or bored?
- Too hot or cold?
- Uncomfortable due to nappy rash, wind etc?

Well-meaning advice

At no other time in your life are you likely to receive more advice than during your first year of parenthood! Everyone – from the health visitor and GP to your mother-in-law and next-door neighbour – will have an opinion on why your baby is crying, and think you want to know about it!

'If you just take their vest off or put a jumper on or feed them or loosen their blanket or turn on the musical mobile or settle them in a quiet room, they will stop crying . . . '

Now, you probably know your baby better than anyone else, so following your instincts is a good place to start. However, sometimes nothing seems to work, or what worked yesterday doesn't work today. Something entirely random may appear to soothe your baby!

Spoiling

Typical phrases you might hear are, 'She's only trying it on!' or 'Don't give in to him!' or 'She'll have you round her little finger' or 'He's just trying to manipulate you!' Another word you may hear cropping up quite often in this well-meaning advice is 'spoil'. 'Don't pick him up every time he cries or you'll spoil him!'

'My mother kept telling me not to pick up the baby when she cried and everyone I spoke to seemed to have a different answer to the age-old problem of what to do to get the baby to sleep more and cry less! I really had no idea what I was doing.'

Pauline, mum to two children (aged one and three).

If you are concerned that responding to your baby every time they cry will 'spoil' them, please be assured that it will not. The research on this matter has shown that it's impossible to spoil a baby. *(Source: Secure and insecure attachments, www.nct.org.uk)*

Remember that babies do not only cry because of their physical needs. They also have social and emotional needs and may cry if they feel alone or frightened.

A rod for your own back?

'Don't hold him all the time, you're only making a rod for your own back!' is another commonly heard piece of advice. The idea here is that if you keep picking your baby up, they will expect it all the time and you won't be able to get anything done. The suggested solution is often to let the baby cry, so they will 'learn how to settle themselves'.

In the short term, this may be true. If a baby's cries are repeatedly ignored they will eventually stop crying as they learn that nothing happens. However, it is important to think about the long-term consequences.

Attachment theory

British psychologist, psychiatrist and psychoanalyst, John Bowlby (1907-1990), developed a theory known as 'attachment theory' (A Secure Base: Parent-Child Attachment and Healthy Human Development, 1988). He suggested that we all need to form close emotional bonds – or attachments – to others and that the quality of this attachment is dependent upon the care we receive as babies.

Secure and insecure attachments

Bowlby suggests that a baby who develops a 'secure attachment' to their carer has learnt to expect a carer who is generally sensitive to their feelings. This does not mean that a parent should rush to their baby's every whim; rather he suggests that parents should be neither too remote nor too over-stimulating.

'With my second baby, I didn't worry about listening to every piece of advice. My second baby also didn't like being put down, was hard to get to go to sleep and woke often for feeds. But I know now that my babies weren't broken and I wasn't doing something wrong.'

Pauline, mum to two children (aged one and three).

According to this theory, if a baby develops an insecure attachment to their carers, they may have problems forming stable relationships as children and adults.

It may sound obvious to state that a child whose parents are insensitive and unresponsive may develop problems with relationships in later life. However, this was a ground-breaking and controversial claim at a time when the upper-middle class believed that parental attention and affection would spoil children.

Pressure on mothers

Bowlby's earlier work on 'maternal deprivation' was used for political purposes to discourage women from working by claiming that any separation from the mother was harmful to the child.

However, Bowlby's attachment theory is not gender specific as babies will form attachments to any consistent caregiver who is sensitive and responsive to their needs. Therefore, there is no reason for the mother to do it all. Babies are equally able to form attachments to fathers and other caregivers.

It is also worth noting that the quality of interaction between carer and baby appears to be more influential then the quantity, so don't think you have to be with your baby every waking minute for them to develop into a stable adult!

Interesting fact

When babies experience stress, they produce high levels of a hormone called cortisol. Research has shown that over time high levels of cortisol can have an adverse impact on brain development. When babies' cries are responded to sensitively, stressful situations become much less likely to provoke such high increases in cortisol.

Source: www.nct.org.uk

Only human

Understanding attachment theory may reassure you when you instinctively want to hold your baby. However, it is important to remember that you are human, and that you, as well as the baby, have needs. Never feel guilty for being 'less than perfect'.

How to comfort and soothe your baby

There are many different ways to soothe a crying baby, and different methods will work for different babies, and at different times. Always start by checking whether they need feeding, winding or changing.

If you think your baby is over-tired but having difficulty sleeping, keep lights and noise to a minimum and take care not to over-stimulate. With the best will in the world, we can sometimes find ourselves rattling things in baby's face, singing, dancing and getting carried away trying to entertain them, when what they really want is some help with switching off!

If you are not sure why your baby is crying, you could try some of the following:

- Holding your baby close to you or carrying in a sling.
- Stroking your baby's back, cheek, tummy etc.
- Holding your baby in different positions.
- Gently rocking your baby in a rocking chair, crib, swing seat or pram.
- Taking your baby out for a walk in their pram or buggy.
- Taking your baby out for a ride in the car (always use a suitable car seat).
- Gently singing, cooing or talking to your baby.
- Playing soft music to your baby and gently swaying and dancing together.
- Trying different types of 'white noise', such as a vacuum cleaner or washing machine.
- Giving your baby a soothing bath, followed by a massage.
- Swaddling – wrapping firmly in a blanket – works for some babies.

'If Aimee is crying for no apparent reason, I hold her close and kiss her on the chin. She also loves it when I sing to her.'

Caroline, mum to Aimee (aged four months).

If you are concerned that your baby is in pain or ill, call the doctor.

Coping with crying

If your baby cries a lot, it can be unbearably stressful and difficult to cope with. If you feel at the end of your tether, there is nothing wrong with putting your baby in a safe place, like a cot or pram, and leaving the room for a few moments to catch your breath. This does not mean that you are being unresponsive or insensitive to your baby or that you are unloving. It is very different from adopting an approach where you choose to leave your baby to cry alone for long periods.

It is important not to struggle on alone. If you have a partner, talk about how you are finding things and what support you might need. If your baby tends to cry a lot in the early evenings, perhaps your partner could try to come home early a few days a week or start work earlier so they can be home earlier to help you through 'colic hour'!

Other parents can also be a tremendous help. Just knowing that your baby is normal and that you are not alone can make things more bearable. We will look further at support in chapter 10.

Summing Up

All babies cry, but some babies cry more than others. There are many different reasons why babies cry, ranging from pain and hunger to boredom and tiredness.

There are many different ways to soothe and comfort a crying baby and different methods will work for different babies, and at different times. Babies love cuddles and being held. Following your instinct is a good place to start.

Coping with a crying baby for long periods of time can be incredibly stressful and it is important to seek support if you are in this situation.

Chapter Four

Sleep

'My hearing changes overnight and I go from someone who could sleep like a log through the heaviest of thunder, to a mummy who'll jump out of her bed at the slightest whimper or change in breathing pattern. Day and night are no longer separated by anything other than the darkness outside.' Extract from the author's journal, written in the first year of motherhood.

Once you become a parent, sleep is never quite the same again! Initially, it can be hard to adjust to night after night of interrupted sleep and you may find yourself going about your daily activities in something of a blur.

However, two things change quite quickly. Firstly, you will adapt to your new sleeping situation and secondly, your baby's sleeping and waking patterns will continue to change over the first year and beyond.

Night feeding

We saw in chapter 2 that a newborn's stomach is only the size of a marble. As young babies' stomachs are so small, they need to be fed regularly to take in sufficient food. Initially, this means they will need to feed during the night.

Babies' sleep patterns

New babies need a lot of sleep to grow and develop, and because their little brains are constantly processing heaps of new information. Although babies sleep a lot, they tend not to do it in one long continuous stretch. Goodbye eight hours' sleep per night!

Babies do not understand that you want them to sleep through the night so you can get some sleep yourself! At first, their sleep patterns may not differ between day and night. They will sleep in short stretches, waking regularly for feeding.

Types of sleep

When humans sleep, they alternate between two main types of sleep:

- Light sleep (REM – Rapid Eye Movement).
- Deep sleep (NREM – Non Rapid Eye Movement).

When we are in light sleep, we tend to wake much more easily, whereas when in deep sleep, we can miraculously sleep through loud noises and disturbances.

Adults spend the majority of their sleeping time in deep sleep. Whereas babies only spend about half of their sleeping time in deep sleep. The rest of the time is spent in light sleep.

As we move from REM to NREM sleep, we wake briefly but rarely remember this. Sometimes, we may get up and use the loo or have a sip of water but often we will simply roll over and go back to sleep. Babies can find it more difficult to go back to sleep when they wake briefly in this way and may quickly become fully awake.

Changing patterns

Gradually, your baby will start to spend more time awake in the day and some form of pattern to their sleeping and waking will emerge. By the time a baby is around three months old, they will usually have started to sleep better at night and developed their own daytime and night-time sleeping patterns.

Of course, as your baby gets older, their sleep patterns will continue to change. This doesn't necessarily develop in a straightforward linear fashion. Your baby may not simply start sleeping less in the day and longer at night. It is important to remember that all sorts of factors may affect your baby's sleep patterns, including weaning and teething.

I was feeling pretty pleased when my son started sleeping through the night at around two months. By 'sleeping through the night', I mean that he slept continuously for a minimum of six hours from around 11.30pm to 5.30am. Six hours' uninterrupted sleep is, by my definition, the minimum amount of uninterrupted sleep that I can reasonably be expected to survive on long term. See how one's expectations can change!

But then when he cut his first tooth, aged eight months, it seemed he didn't sleep again for the next year. Then he became a toddler and experienced separation anxiety. Not to mention all the bouts of coughs and colds and stomach upsets and high temperatures and eczema and the rest of it. You get the picture.

When I was a new mum, I used to hear these stories of six-week-old babies sleeping twelve hours a night without so much as a peep. If you have one of these mythical creatures, lucky you! For the rest of us, don't worry. You will learn to cope. And always remember the new parent's mantra that I mentioned previously: This too *will* pass. Eventually . . .

Coping with interrupted sleep

In the early days, you might want to try to sleep when the baby sleeps. If you have been up a lot in the night with your baby, a daytime nap can be helpful for you to catch up on your own sleep and restore your energy. So when your baby drops off for a daytime nap, put your feet up and rest too.

Looking after a new baby is physically and mentally exhausting. It is important that you get plenty of rest, so never feel guilty about sleeping in the day, even if you haven't washed the breakfast dishes yet . . . so what? It can be hard to explain to a non-parent how all-consuming new baby care is, but all new parents understand how tired you get.

'It helps to take a rest with the children when I need to and know my limits by not packing too much into the day as we all get very exhausted.'

Avvai, mum to two children (aged one and four).

Sleep is not a competition

It might sound like a strange thing to say, but at times it can feel as though when you become a parent, you are automatically entered into a series of competitions. Whose baby sleeps the longest? Ta da, gold trophy to the mummy in the front row. Whose baby crawls first? Clever you, have a gold star.

It is natural to seek reassurance from other parents by talking about your baby and their developmental milestones. Inevitable then, that you may find yourself comparing your baby to the baby next door, who of course, will be 'perfect' in every way. It is all too easy to get sucked into competitive parenting, where parents try to outdo each other by having the baby who sleeps the longest, cries the least, and does everything the 'textbooks' say they should be doing.

It is completely pointless and a total waste of your emotional energy. Your baby is who they are. They will sleep when they need to sleep, eat when they need to eat, cry when they need to tell you something. They will develop in their own unique ways, at their own pace. All babies are perfect in their own way.

Where should your baby sleep?

Health visitors currently advise that babies sleep in the same room as their parents until they are six months old, to help reduce the risk of cot death.

Your baby may sleep in a Moses basket, a crib, a cot or a cotbed, or they may share your bed. Many factors will influence your decision, including space, finances, your child's sleep patterns and needs, and your parenting philosophy.

Positioning in the bed

The safest position for your baby to sleep in is on their back. Position your baby with their feet at the bottom of the basket or cot so that they cannot wriggle down under the covers.

'Coping with uninterrupted sleep and everything is tough . . . try to remind yourself it won't be like this forever. Babies grow up so fast. Also, no matter what, get some time to yourself every day if you can - even if it is only for 20 minutes, it's really important.'

Caroline, mum to Aimee (aged four months).

Co-sleeping

Some parents opt for co-sleeping from birth as a planned parenting choice. Co-sleeping – also known as the 'family bed approach' – is a key part of some parenting philosophies, such as 'attachment parenting'. *(Source: www. attachmentparenting.org)* Co-sleeping is one way in which parents may practice 'proximal care', which basically means keeping your baby in close proximity.

In Western society, we put a lot of value on independence. This can put pressure on parents to feel that they are not 'doing things right' if their child is not sleeping alone. However, in many other cultures where proximal care is practised, it is usual practice for babies and young children to sleep with their parents.

As planned co-sleeping is a minority practice in Western society, if you do choose to co-sleep, you may find that you come up with some resistance from other people. Remember that if you and your child are happy and getting enough sleep, it really is nobody else's business.

Safety

The Department of Health advises against co-sleeping with a baby if one or both parents:

- Smokes.
- Has used alcohol or drugs (including prescription drugs) that affect perception, cause drowsiness or affect depth of sleep.
- Is excessively tired to the extent that this might affect being able to respond to the baby.

'All a baby wants is to feel warm and safe and snugly and be fed when they are hungry. They have been in a warm, dark cocoon for nine months and it must be so strange and scary when they are born, to be let out in this cold, bright, noisy environment.'

Avvai, mum to two children (aged one and four).

No right or wrong way

All families are different, and this includes babies as well as parents. Some babies just don't seem to settle unless they are constantly in physical contact with their caregivers. However, other babies may seem perfectly content to sleep alone and easily settle themselves to sleep. Some parents are happy to have their babies in bed with them, but others do not consider this an option.

If you only take away one thing from this book, I hope it will be to always do what feels right for your family. There is no one right way to do it!

I would also encourage you to take what you need from different approaches, rather than feel you have to adopt a particular philosophy 'wholesale'. Feeling that you 'should' be following any one particular parenting philosophy unquestioning, can become oppressive. This can be equally true of more 'liberal' parenting styles as it is of 'routine-based' approaches.

Perhaps you want to breastfeed on demand but you don't like the thought of co-sleeping, or vice versa. Perhaps you believe in proximal care but feel that some routine is important to you. It doesn't have to be all or nothing! Just go with what feels right instinctively.

'Leila hardly slept during the day until she started to crawl. As with most things I've been completely led by her, I've never tried to impose regular daytime naps and now she'll sometimes have a morning nap and an afternoon nap, and sometimes she'll have a monster nap in the middle of the day.'

Dawn, mum to Leila (aged 10 months).

Case study

Avvai is a mother to two young children, aged one and four years. Avvai adopts a baby-led approach to parenting, where she is led by her children. The approach works by taking cues from the baby and responding to them, rather than parenting to a schedule.

As an advocate of co-sleeping, baby wearing and breastfeeding on demand, Avvai says that she has not had to do much soothing of a crying baby as she is always on hand.

The children do have a bedtime routine but daytime sleep patterns vary each day/week depending on what stimulus they have had during the day. These nap patterns have been led by the children.

Avvai says that there is huge difference in information and support for co-sleeping now compared to when she had her first baby: 'There are so many more mums aware of baby-led parenting and you are not perceived as some hippy with outlandish ways of child rearing . . . it is becoming more mainstream.'

'The only structure I have in the day is bedtime, which tends to be a bath followed by a baby massage, soft music, lavender and milk and a book.'

Avvai, mum to two children (aged one and four).

Sleep routines

A relaxing night-time routine can assist greatly in establishing a peaceful bedtime, which is conducive to sleep. A typical bedtime routine might consist of having a warm bath, changing into bedclothes, breast or bottle feeding, sharing a story and then going to sleep.

Going to bed at around the same time each night can help your baby establish a regular sleep pattern, anticipate what is coming next and wind down for sleep. Some babies also settle into regular daytime naps, whereas other babies' patterns vary. In any event, your baby's sleep pattern will change as they develop.

Bedtimes

Babies' bedtimes can vary enormously and like everything else, there is no wrong or right way. A common bedtime for a baby seems to be around 7pm. However, young babies are often fretful in the evening, particularly if they suffer from colic, and may not settle until later. If your baby is sleeping a lot during the day or simply needs less sleep than average, a considerably later bedtime is not inappropriate.

Some parents prefer to keep their baby up later in the hope that they will be so tired that they will sleep better/longer/later. However, you should be warned that this can backfire as an over-tired, over-stimulated baby may have a more fitful night's sleep.

Settling

There are different ways to settle a fretful baby, as discussed in the previous chapter. Many parents worry that if they feed/rock/cuddle their babies to sleep, the baby will expect this all the time and it will become unmanageable.

Another approach is to encourage the baby to sleep alone by placing them in their basket or cot and singing/talking/patting them while they are in the cot rather than picking them up. Some babies respond well to this.

Dummies

Research has suggested that using a dummy at the start of any sleep period may reduce the risk of cot death. If you are breastfeeding, it's best not to use a dummy for the first month as it may interfere with establishing feeding. (*Source: Cot death: how to reduce the risks, www.nhs.co.uk*) Some babies love dummies and others don't take to them at all. Always be led by your baby.

Summing Up

Coping with interrupted night-time sleep can take some getting used to, but you will adapt. Try to have a rest when your baby rests so you don't get too worn out.

At first, your baby will probably sleep in short stretches in the day and night, and wake regularly for feeding. Newborn babies spend about half of their sleeping time in light sleep and may wake easily and need help to settle. Their sleep patterns will continue to change throughout the first year and will be influenced by a range of factors, including teething and weaning.

Try not to compare your baby's sleeping habits to other babies'. Remember that sleep is not a competition!

Chapter Five

Keeping Baby Clean

'Winding invariably resulted in sticky baby posset missing the muslin cloth draped over my shoulder and landing on my hair. Then Smallboy would moan and strain and produce an astonishing amount of poo, which managed to find its way up the back of his Babygro despite the "leak proof" nappy.' Extract from the author's journal, written in the first year of motherhood.

Keeping your new baby clean can sometimes feel like a rather tricky process! What with baby bringing up milk (known as 'possetting') at one end and filling their nappy at the other end, early days of parenthood can feel like one long round of cleaning and changing!

Bathing

If you gave birth in hospital, you will have probably been shown how to bathe your baby by a midwife. If you haven't been shown, don't panic! It's really very simple.

What you need

The basic equipment that you will need to bathe your baby is:

- Baby bath or bath aid to use in main bath.
- Baby sponge or flannel.
- Soft towel.

And that's it! Plain water is sufficient for newborns. They don't need bubble bath or soap, which can irritate their delicate skin.

Baby baths

You can buy a range of specially designed baby baths suitable for use with babies at different ages. The classic newborn baby bath is simply a mini plastic bath with a sloping end, that you fill with water and empty after use.

Some models come with their own plug hole to make emptying easier, particularly if you place it in the main bath during use. With others you simply tip the water out. If you are not using the baby bath within the main bath, it is important to ensure that you place it on a secure, non-slip surface.

You can also buy 'over the bath' baby baths, which fit on top of your bath so you don't have to lean over and into the bath. Alternatively, all-in-one bath and changing units are available, with an integral baby bath on top of a changing unit. This is ideal if you prefer to perform baby care tasks standing up.

Bath aids

If you would prefer to bath your baby in the main household bath from day one, you might like to consider purchasing a bath aid to use in the bath. For newborns, you can get reclining plastic supports for your baby. As your baby gets older and can sit up, you can move onto a bath seat, such as a ring style bath seat.

Some mums and dads might prefer to get in the bath with the baby and have a bath together. Just remember to make sure the temperature is right for your baby!

Baby towels

You can buy baby towels with integral hoods (often featuring animal ears!) to help keep baby's head warm and dry after bathing. You can also buy towels which attach to the parent like an apron, making it easier to manoeuvre your baby out of the bath and into the towel. However, you don't really need to spend a lot of money on gimmicky towels if you don't want to. Any soft towel will do.

Temperature

You only need a few inches of warm water for a newborn. The temperature of the water should be between 36-37°C. You can buy a special baby bath thermometer to help you check the temperature. Some parents prefer to test the temperature the old-fashioned way by dipping their elbow into the water. It is good practice to put the cold water into the bath first and then add the hot, mixing thoroughly. This helps to prevent the risk of making the bath too hot.

How to bathe your baby

It can be a good idea to warm the towel before you start so your baby doesn't experience any unwelcome shocks! It's easier to wash your baby's face and bottom with cotton wool and plain water before you put them in the bath.

Newborns have a weak immune system, so to reduce the risk of infections, it's best to use cooled boiled water, with separate pieces of cotton wool for each eye, around the nose and mouth, and the creases in the neck.

The usual way to bath a baby is to support your baby's head and back with one arm and use the other hand to wash your baby. Remember that young babies don't need that much washing!

Dry your baby carefully with the warm towel using a gentle patting motion and making sure you get into all the creases in baby's skin. Take care with the area around the umbilical cord and the soft spots (fontanelles) on your baby's head.

Safety

Remember that babies can drown even in a few inches of water. Never leave your baby alone in the bath. If you are called away from the bath, take your baby out, wrap them in a towel and take them with you.

'When I'm bathing Aimee, I use a sponge support so she feels secure yet has the opportunity to kick and splash. I make sure she doesn't get splashed on the face and always have the towel ready so she doesn't get cold before or after the bath.'

Caroline, mum to Aimee (aged four months).

Top and tail

Your baby doesn't really need a bath every day. The important bits to keep clean are their face and nappy area! This can easily be achieved by 'topping and tailing', which basically means laying your baby on a changing mat and just washing the face, genital area and bottom. If your baby isn't having a bath, be sure to wash their hands when you do the top and tail.

Nappy changing

Interesting fact

During baby's first year, it is estimated that you will need to change your baby's nappy 2,788 times! That's a whole lot of nappy changes!

Source: www.kgbanswers.com

A key decision that you will need to make is whether to buy reusable nappies or disposable ones.

Reusable Vs disposable

There are lots of arguments for and against reusable nappies and disposable nappies. The main arguments for using reusable, washable nappies are that long term they work out cheaper and are better for the environment. However, some people argue that once you have factored in all the washing required, the benefit to the environment may not be as great as people think.

Interestingly, an updated lifecycle assessment study for disposable and reusable nappies by the UK Environment Agency and Department for Environment, Food and Rural Affairs (DEFRA), found that reusable nappies can cause either more or less damage to the environment than disposable ones, depending on how they are washed and dried.

To help save the environment, parents choosing reusable nappies should consider:

▪ Not washing above 60°C (140°F).

- Washing fuller loads.
- Line drying rather than tumble drying nappies whenever possible.
- Choosing more energy-efficient washing machines.
- Reusing nappies on other children.

The main argument for using disposable nappies is convenience. Some people also believe that disposables are more comfortable for baby than washable nappies, and keep baby drier, which helps to prevent nappy rash. However, as modern reusable nappies are now available in a variety of materials and types, this may or may not be true for your baby.

You will need to weigh everything up and make a decision based on what you think will work best for you and your family. Of course, you can change your mind at any time! You might start out with disposables and then switch to reusables once your baby is a little older, for instance. Or you may decide to mix both types, perhaps using disposables at night-time and/or when you are out and about and reusables for daytime/home use.

Some local authorities have reusable nappy schemes, which will supply a regular batch of clean washable nappies and collect soiled nappies from you for a fixed price. This saves you the trouble of having to wash the nappies yourself and therefore provides greater convenience. You can enquire at your local council to see if this service is available in your area.

Types of disposable nappies

Disposable nappies come in a startling array of brands and types. Standard disposables have an absorbent inner layer and waterproof outer layer and are secured with adhesive tabs at either side. They usually have elasticated legs to help prevent leaks. Some are deemed 'eco-nappies' and are supposedly better for the environment because they are made of biodegradable materials which naturally break down.

Disposables come in sizes to fit newborns up to toddlers, and are usually labelled according to baby's weight. Special 'night-time' nappies are also available which are supposed to hold liquid for longer than standard nappies, and therefore keep baby drier for longer.

Soiled nappies should be disposed of with household waste, never down the toilet. You can wrap the nappy in a 'nappy sack' first if you prefer, which helps contain the contents and eliminate odour.

Types of reusable nappies

There are two main types of reusable nappies, as follows:

- Traditional terry towelling cloth nappies, square or T-shaped which you fold and secure with a nappy pin, and use with separate waterproof pants or wrapper.
- All-in-one shaped nappies, with integral padding and wrapper, which come in a variety of styles and sizes.

Terry towelling cloths are the cheaper option, whereas the all-in-one nappies, while expensive, provide greater convenience. If you're using terry nappies, you will only need to buy a few wrappers, as you can use the same wrapper all day, as long as it is not directly soiled.

All-in-ones are available in 'one size fits all' adjustable nappies, which will last for the whole of the baby's nappy-wearing time. Alternatively, you can get all-in-ones in a range of different sizes, which you will need to replace as your baby grows.

Nappy liners and padding

When using reusable nappies, you will usually need to use the following (even with the 'all-in-one' versions):

- Nappy liners which remain dry next to baby's skin and make it easier to remove baby poo.
- Additional absorbency padding to prevent leaks.

Nappy liners are strong and tissue-like, and can be made of various materials, such as paper or even silk. Flushable versions are available.

'My daughter has done some seriously squishy poos and her reusable nappies have not leaked. She's also had some long outings in them without leaks. In fact, she wears reusables at night, too, with no problems.'

Rachel, mum to two daughters (aged one and three) with baby number three on the way.

Padding, also known as 'nappy pads', 'diaper doublers' and 'nappy boosters', is available in a wide range of types and materials (man-made or natural), and can be disposable or washable.

Case study

Rachel Pattisson is mum to two young daughters, with baby number three on the way. After years of using eco-disposable nappies, Rachel decided to give reusables a try. Rachel says that making the decision to use reusable nappies was the easy part. Choosing between the plethora of different styles and brands of washable nappies was confusing, to say the least.

Luckily, Rachel was able to borrow some reusables from a friend, to try them out. If you have a friend who will do this for you, it is an excellent idea. By borrowing some nappies, you can get an idea of what type is right for your family and, more importantly, whether the whole washable nappy 'thing' will work for you. If you haven't got a friend who will lend you some nappies, you could try sourcing nappies second hand from www.thenappysite.co.uk.

Rachel says it is important not to be put off by the range of choice. She has tried shaped terry nappies as well as one-size nappies with integral waterproof layer and found that both types worked well. She loved the convenience (yes, you read that right!) of washable nappies so much that she bought her own.

Rachel blogs about motherhood at http://rachelpattisson.blogspot.com

'Some torn up strips of old towels provide additional absorbency without the added price-tag. I have been successfully using one "bought" booster and one strip of towelling in each of my daughter's nappies, which certainly cuts down on the expense of extra boosters.'

Rachel, mum to two daughters (aged one and three) with baby number three on the way.

How and when to change a nappy

When to change

There are no prescriptive times to change a nappy but try not to leave your baby in a dirty nappy. The important thing is to keep your baby clean and comfortable. Sensible times to change a nappy are:

- On waking in the morning.
- After every feed.
- After bath time.
- At bedtime.
- And whenever you notice that the nappy is soiled or wet.

Where to change

It's best to change your baby's nappy on a soft, waterproof changing mat and in a warm room. Changing mats can be placed on the floor or bed or on a changing table. As your baby gets older and starts wriggling and rolling, you will need to be careful that they cannot roll off of the surface.

How to change

It's easiest to have everything to hand that you will need. You can clean your baby with a baby wipe or wet cotton wool (the latter is generally kinder on sensitive skin and therefore recommended for newborns). If your baby has done a poo, wet cotton wool alone may not be enough, so you may wish to use a little baby lotion.

The general nappy changing sequence for (disposables or reusables) is as follows:

- Remove baby's dirty nappy.
- Clean baby's genital area, bottom and top of legs.

- Put on a clean nappy.
- Dress your baby.
- Ensure your baby is in a safe place while you dispose of or store the dirty nappy.
- Wash your hands.

Always wipe a baby girl from front to back to avoid the spread of bacteria and prevent infection.

Baby boys have a tendency to do a wee just as you take the nappy off, so to avoid getting soaked, have a cotton wool ball ready to hold over your little boy's penis as soon as you take his nappy off!

Easy to remove clothing

You might find it helpful to use easy to remove clothing, particularly in the early weeks and months when your baby will need changing regularly. Poppers are generally easier to manage than buttons. Avoid the type of Babygro which needs to be completely removed every time you need to change a nappy. Opt for clothing which allows you to easily remove the bottom half only.

Nappy rash

Keeping baby clean and dry is the best way to help reduce the risk of nappy rash. This means changing your baby's nappy regularly. Nappy liners can also help. You can also apply a specially formulated barrier cream to help prevent nappy rash before putting on the nappy.

Let your baby's bottom get a regular airing by allowing your baby to have a kick around on the changing mat before you put the next nappy on.

Summing Up

You can bathe your baby in a baby bath or in the main bath, using a bath support. Always check the water temperature before putting your baby in the bath, and never leave your baby unattended in the bath. Babies don't need to have a bath every day; you can top and tail for convenience.

When deciding what type of nappy to use, you will need to weigh up the pros and cons of disposable and reusable nappies. It is a good idea to try both out before making up your mind. Many local authorities run reusable nappy schemes.

Chapter Six
Baby's Development

'"He's not showing any signs of crawling," I confided to my neighbour when my son reached six months, the textbook age for baby to start getting mobile. "Oh, mine never crawled," she consoled. "The first one was a bottom shuffler and the second had this funny one-legged wiggle."' Extract from the author's journal, written in the first year of motherhood.

During your baby's first year, they will go through huge physical changes as their bodies and minds grow and develop. One of the most exciting things about being a parent is watching your baby conquer a new skill for the first time, from rolling over and sitting up, to crawling (or shuffling or wiggling) and walking.

All babies develop differently and at different rates, so it is impossible to predict exactly what your baby will be doing and when. My son never went through the crawling stage at all. At the time, I worried about what I perceived to be his unusual development.

Comparing your baby's development to other babies' can get you in a pickle if you are expecting them all to develop in the same way. However, it can be helpful to have a rough idea of the average baby's physical development and what you might expect. Remember though, that the 'average baby' is a theoretical statistic, and your baby is a real live person with all the quirks and eccentricities that make them unique!

Brain and body

Your baby's brain and body are developing rapidly week by week. The increasing skills and co-ordination needed to roll, sit, crawl, stand and then walk are controlled by a combination of strengthening muscles and a developing brain and nervous system.

Vision

Your newborn baby's vision is limited and initially they can only distinguish between very bright colours such as red and blue. Make sure you have brightly coloured toys around your baby, such as cot toys and hanging mobiles.

Initially, your baby's range of vision is fairly restricted and they can only focus on things within about 30 centimetres' range. Your baby's eyes will, however, be sensitive to the human face, particularly the face of his primary caregivers, so it is a good idea to hold your face close to your baby when you talk to them. Your baby will react to your smile and facial expressions.

It usually takes until about four to six months for babies to be able to see fully in three-dimensions.

Checking eyesight

By the age of four months, your baby should be able to focus on a brightly coloured object held about 20-25 centimetres from their face and follow it with their eyes if you move it. If you have any concerns, talk to your health visitor or doctor.

Hand-eye co-ordination

Co-ordination is important for a whole range of activities and movements and something that your baby will continually develop during their first year.

By about two months of age, your baby will begin to try to control their hand movements. They will learn about hand movement by watching their hands and coming to realise that they can control this movement. Before this stage, a baby's grip is down to an involuntary grasp reflex, which can feel very strong.

Hand-eye co-ordination develops gradually and at first your baby will spend a lot of time simply looking at their hands and opening and closing them. By about four months, a baby usually begins to be able to reach and grab for objects. At around six months, they may be able to hold an object and will enjoy feeling different textures.

'We had a baby playmat and gym so we laid him down on it fairly early on. At first he would just look at the colours and characters hanging from the arches, but soon he tried to touch them, encouraged and congratulated by us the whole time.'

Agnes, mum to Edgar (aged 10 months).

By about eight months, your baby will probably be able to hold an object out to you but not be able to let go. By around their first birthday, they will have learned how to drop things and enjoy watching them fall! Get your mop ready!

Rolling

Your baby will gradually develop the strength and co-ordination needed to roll. Most babies can roll by around four to five months, but don't worry if it takes longer.

Sitting

Your baby will need to develop muscles in their neck, shoulders and torso before they can start to sit without support (usually around six to eight months). However, you can prop your baby up in a sitting position using cushions before this, as long as they are well supported.

Many babies also enjoy 'sitting' in a baby bouncer. There are many different types on the market, from basic models to all-singing, all-dancing models which swing/vibrate/play tunes/cook your dinner! (I'm joking about the last bit!) Above all else, your baby will enjoy being able to observe what is going on around them while in a semi-upright position. Even if this is just you cooking the dinner, to baby it's entertainment!

'With his hands being naturally tightly closed at the beginning, we would put a small rattly soft toy in one of them, and he would move his arm, still holding on tight to the toy, making it rattle. We would encourage and congratulate him and he seemed to be amazed that he was making it move on his own.'

Agnes, mum to Edgar (aged 10 months).

Crawling

> **Interesting fact**
>
> Some babies never crawl at all, but still manage to learn to walk perfectly well.

Some babies (mine included) never crawl at all, but still manage to learn to walk perfectly well. If your baby is going to crawl, they will probably start to do so by around eight or nine months, although it may be later than this.

In theory, it is supposed to be helpful if you lie your baby on their tummy but some babies (yes, mine included) don't always seem to like this very much and prefer to be upright, seeing what is going on around them.

Standing

By nine or ten months, your baby will probably enjoy being supported in a standing position. My son liked being held upright from a very young age. By around ten months, your baby may start pulling themselves to standing, using the sofa, for example.

Don't worry if your baby takes longer to show an interest. All babies are different. When your baby does start to show an interest in standing, it is a good idea to allow them to go barefoot.

First steps

Once your baby has mastered pulling themselves up, grabbing hold of whatever is nearby, they will probably enjoy 'cruising' or edging themselves along holding onto furniture etc.

Gradually, they will start attempting to walk over to the next thing they can grab hold of, perhaps taking their first unaided step between the sofa and table! As they gain confidence, they will get braver. One day, you'll look up and see your baby making a dash for it and you won't believe your eyes!

Never try to rush the process. Your baby is ready when they are ready.

Baby sounds

Initially, the main sound you will hear from your baby will be crying, but they will gradually develop a range of baby sounds, including cooing. Some babies can start saying 'Ma', 'Da' then 'Mama' and 'Dada' (oh the joy) from as early as six to seven months. Don't be too upset if your baby says 'Dada' first or vice versa!

Your baby will develop their baby babble rapidly and try to imitate your speech. By the end of baby's first year, they might start to say their first 'real words' such as 'dog' or 'cat'. Your baby's own first words will probably be particular to the things they like and see and do regularly.

Additional needs

Of course, all babies are unique and special in their own ways. Some babies may be born with or develop medical conditions or physical or intellectual disabilities which mean that their physical and/or intellectual development follows a different path than others.

If your baby has additional needs, it is important that you access support and information that is appropriate to your child's needs. This will help you to understand your child's needs and any adjustments that you may need to make to family life and parenting to fully accommodate those needs.

It can also be tremendously reassuring to talk to other parents whose children share the same condition to find out how they have coped and share milestones. A good starting point is UK charity Contact a Family (see the useful organisations list).

'Because Aimee has Down's syndrome, the biggest challenge for us so far was dealing with that issue. Every day the challenge gets easier to deal with because she is in great health and just like any other baby.'

Caroline, mum to Aimee (aged four months).

Case study

Caroline lives with her husband and daughter Aimee (aged four months) in Ireland. The early intervention team in the Carlow/Kilkenny region where they live meet regularly and discuss Aimee's progress (as well as all the Down's syndrome children in the region). The team consists of a paediatrician, physiotherapist, occupational therapist, speech and language therapist and public health nurse. These services are automatically available to children born with Down's syndrome in this region. Details of these services are provided by the specialist public health nurse who gets in touch with new parents in the first few weeks after birth.

Caroline says that the services provided in her area have helped the whole family deal with their daughter having Down's syndrome. Also, meeting other parents in the same situation has been particularly helpful.

Health and illness

Of course, all babies get ill sometimes. This is a natural part of life. Because babies and young children have much weaker immune systems than adults, they can be susceptible to picking up infections easily.

Fever

Babies with viral or bacterial infections will often run a high temperature or fever. Normal body temperature is 36-37°C. A temperature over 37.5°C is classified as a fever. Fever can be dangerous for babies and there can be risks of a convulsion if the temperature is not reduced.

Fever can be reduced with age-appropriate paracetamol medicine (such as Calpol). Always check suitability with a pharmacist or doctor. You can also reduce temperature by removing your child's clothing and sponging them with tepid water.

You should consult your doctor straight away if:

- Your baby is under six months old and has a fever.
- A fever lasts for more than 24 hours.
- Your baby has a convulsion.
- You are worried.

Seeking medical advice

If you have any concerns over your baby's health or their development at any time, always consult your doctor and/or health visitor at the earliest opportunity.

Immunisations

Your health visitor will advise you of recommended immunisations for your baby to protect against a range of infectious diseases. There may be some minor side effects to some immunisations for some babies, which your health visitor or doctor can advise you on. Generally, the risk of complications from immunisations is significantly smaller than the risks associated with your child contracting the disease.

Summing Up

During your baby's first year, you will notice many changes as they grow and develop from a tiny helpless newborn to a mobile, communicative toddler. They will develop their skills and co-ordination as their muscles strengthen and their brain and nervous system develop.

All babies develop slightly differently, so don't worry if your baby is not doing things in the same order or at the same speed as other babies. If you do have any concerns about your baby's health or development, speak to your health visitor or doctor.

Chapter Seven

Teething

'Tuesday the 13th February: My baby cut his first tooth, aged eight months. It seemed he didn't sleep again for the next year as one after one, the pointy raggedy stones erupted out of his gums.' Extract from the author's journal, written in the first year of motherhood.

Cutting their first tooth is another major milestone in baby's first year, and you might find yourself constantly checking your baby's mouth for any sign of action. It is impossible to predict when your baby will start teething, but believe me they will let you know!

Babies normally develop their 'milk teeth' while in the womb and some babies are actually born with one or more teeth already emerged through the gums. The average age to start teething is around six months but some babies still haven't got any teeth by one year.

Before your baby cuts their first tooth, you will probably notice that they are dribbling a lot more than usual. They may also be chewing everything in sight and seem clingy and upset. As each tooth starts to push through your baby's gums, you will notice a pale bump, before a tiny sharp point erupts.

Teething can be very painful for babies and they don't understand what is going on, which makes it difficult for them to cope. This can mean a lot of crying and sleepless nights, which, of course, can make it difficult for you too!

However, there are ways that you can help soothe your baby during the teething process, and remember, like all challenges of parenting, this is just a temporary phase.

Stages of teething

Although teething starts at different times for different babies, the order that the teeth come through is usually the same. During baby's first year, they are likely to develop the following teeth in this order:

- Bottom incisors (front two teeth).
- Top incisors (front two teeth).
- Top lateral incisors (either side of the top front teeth).
- Bottom lateral incisors (either side of the bottom front teeth).

The molars (back teeth) usually start erupting some time at the beginning of baby's second year. The full teething process – twenty milk teeth – is normally completed by around two and a half years.

Soothing teething pain

There are many different things that you can try to help soothe your baby's teething pain, such as giving them something hard and cold to chew on, rubbing their gums with your finger, and using teething gels or powders.

The most important thing is to provide comfort to your baby when they are going through this difficult time. They are likely to want lots of extra cuddles. Try to find ways to distract them from their pain but don't be surprised if they are too irritable to entertain your ideas!

Teething gels

You can buy sugar-free teething gel suitable for babies over four months of age. You can also buy different types of teething powders, including herbal powders. If you are unsure about using them or worried about the possible side effects, talk to your doctor or health visitor.

'We used Calpol and Bonjela to help relieve the pain and just made sure they wore a bib all the time.'

Vusi, mum to William (aged eight months), Thomas (aged twenty months) and Charlie (aged five years).

Teething rings

You can buy a range of teething aids, such as teething rings and other teething toys, which your baby can safely chew on. Some teething aids are designed to be put in the fridge to cool them down prior to use. It is not advisable to put them in the freezer as they will get too cold and could damage your baby's delicate gums.

Old-fashioned remedies

A cold wet cloth is a good alternative to a teething ring. You can also put raw carrots in the fridge and then give them to your baby to chew on. Chewing on crusty bread can help some babies and can be a useful alternative to baby 'rusks' which usually contain sugar.

Case study

Vusi, mum to three boys, is currently going through teething for the third time, with her youngest son, William, aged eight months. Vusi acknowledges how difficult it is to see your child in obvious pain during the teething process but having been through it twice before, she is well prepared! With all three boys, Vusi has used teething gel to help relieve the pain.

She tried cold cucumber with her first two sons, but both Charlie and Thomas had such a strong bite that they would bite little bits off, so they stuck with really firm cold carrots, a cold wet cloth and teethings toys that had been in the fridge. Vusi says that the cold wet cloth seemed to be the best method and William seems to favour that one as well.

She also makes sure William wears a bib all the time to protect against the constant dribbling. As Vusi's own mum is a health visitor, the family have had a constant source of support. The only thing the family have done differently with William, is not to use cold cucumber!

'We tried cold cucumber, but both Charlie and Thomas had such a strong bite that we stuck with really firm cold carrots, a cold wet cloth and teethings toys that had been in the fridge.'

Vusi, mum to William (aged eight months), Thomas (aged twenty months) and Charlie (aged five years).

Looking after first teeth

Cleaning your baby's teeth

It is never too early to introduce the toothbrush! Let your baby watch you brush your teeth morning and night so they get the general idea and want to copy you. Offer a soft first toothbrush to your baby to hold and play with. They will probably chew on it rather than engage in actual brushing, but it is all part of the process.

As soon as your baby's first teeth come in, they will need to be cleaned regularly using a smear of toothpaste. Gently brush them for your baby with a baby toothbrush.

Your baby's diet

You will be looking at your baby's diet in chapter 9 – Weaning, but it goes without saying that one of the best ways to strengthen and protect your baby's developing teeth is to ensure that they have a good diet. Calcium and vitamin D are important for the formation of your baby's permanent teeth, which are already growing in your baby's jawbones.

Sugary foods are obviously not a good idea for a baby. Even constantly sipping fruit juice can be a threat to your baby's teeth, because of the natural sugars and acid in the juice. It is a good idea to generally only offer juice with food at mealtimes and not allow your baby to sip juice from a bottle throughout the day. When your baby is weaning, water is a perfectly adequate drink to have in addition to milk.

Summing Up

Most babies start teething around the six month mark, although some are born with teeth and others are still gummy at the end of their first year. The complete teething process – twenty milk teeth – usually takes until they are around two and a half years old.

You may notice signs of teething, such as excessive dribbling and being clingy or upset. There are various ways that you can help soothe your baby's teething pain, including teething rings and gels, as well as more old-fashioned remedies such as chewing on a cold carrot. As soon as your baby has any teeth, they will need to be cleaned regularly.

Chapter Eight

Interaction and Play

'Smallboy might not be able to speak but he certainly lets us know what he thinks . . . He chose his own highchair by flapping his arms and legs about and squawking. We ended up with the lurid neon plastic one not the trendy wooden one we wanted!' Extract from the author's journal, written in the first year of motherhood.

How babies communicate

Pre-verbal babies have a range of ways of communicating. Crying is the most obvious method, but there are many more ways that babies can interact.

Eye contact

Eye contact and facial expressions are important ways of communicating. If you look directly at your baby and pull different expressions, they are likely to start copying you. And of course, smiling and laughing are also very contagious.

Body language

Babies can also communicate their feelings, wishes and needs via body language. This could be as simple as waving their limbs in the air when they are excited, or as sophisticated as pointing to a toy or item of food that they would like you to pass them.

Expressing feelings, needs and wants

When our son was a baby, he used to make his feelings plain by expressing himself through sounds and movement. He even chose his own highchair this way. I marched into the baby store, carried him up and down the aisle and dangled him over various highchairs, jabbering on asking him which one he liked.

He looked on in amusement, flapping his arms and legs about and squawking. When we reached one that elicited a particularly high amount of flapping, I sat him in it for size. It was a stylish wooden number that would go well in the dining room. You know the type: comes with a choice of fabric cushion to suit every interior, can be adapted into a dining chair to provide longevity of use, some even morph into table and chair combo, all are very nice.

Smallboy slumped down in it and looked miserable. We tried again. This time, he went crazy in front of a huge lurid neon animal patterned padded plastic monstrosity that I really didn't want in my house. I sat him in it. You guessed it; he patted his hands on the plastic tray and started laughing.

The baby-parent dance

The baby-parent dance refers to the process of baby and parent responding to one another's rhythms. Taking cues from your baby is a great way of pacing your interaction and play. Sometimes, your baby will be very lively and want a lot of interaction. At other times, they may be over-stimulated and not want to engage. Perhaps they will show you by turning away or crying.

The social baby

Babies are social animals. They enjoy the company of others. Mummy and Daddy are naturally their favourite playthings. Other children will also be of immense interest.

Meeting up with other parents with babies can be a good way to introduce your baby to company and for you to get some much needed adult conversation into the bargain! You can speak to your health visitor for information on parent and baby groups in your area.

Need2Know

Parent and baby activities can be as simple as a weekly coffee morning. You can also try structured activities such as parent-baby swimming classes, baby yoga or baby massage.

Some babies enjoy doing lots of different things, whereas others become over-stimulated more easily and tire quickly. Always take cues from your baby rather than do what you think you 'should' be doing. There is no point running around trying to keep up with a hectic schedule if your baby is miserable and would rather be at home, having quiet time with you! You know your baby better than anyone else.

Case study

Agnes and her husband have been playing with their son Edgar since birth. Initially, they sang songs that involved tickling or touching him, or miming. Agnes says, 'We would shake a muslin cloth over his face or nose, making high-pitched noises with the movement of the muslin, to which he would happily react.'

Baby Edgar also enjoyed lying on a baby gym, first looking at the hanging toys and then trying to touch them. Agnes says that Edgar soon learned to smile and make contented sounds, and even later on he would giggle. Agnes believes that play and interaction is so important to make a baby feel valued and loved.

Edgar started as a spectator to his parents' games but as he has grown, he has begun to initiate games and become more involved. Now that he is 10 months old, Edgar plays on his own more (with Mum or Dad nearby to give him a smile or a word and make sure he doesn't get up to mischief!). He loves exploring and trying things on his own and will happily sit for half an hour concentrating on whatever game he's invented.

Edgar also seems absolutely captivated by books and enjoys being taken out for a walk or to the playground, dancing, swimming and singing.

Baby massage

Baby massage can be a really good way of bonding through touch with your baby. Many local councils offer sessions for parent and baby to attend, for a small fee. There are also private service providers offering classes, which may be more expensive.

Of course, you don't need to attend classes to massage your baby. You could simply go with the flow and see what your baby likes. However, it can be handy to see techniques demonstrated and find out which techniques may be helpful for particular issues, e.g. indigestion, constipation, settling to sleep etc.

Play and learning

Everything your baby does facilitates their learning about themselves and the world around them. During baby's first year, they will learn more rapidly than any other time in their lives. Every new experience presents a learning opportunity and your baby will be processing an enormous amount of information every day.

Through play, your baby will learn communication skills, develop their physical co-ordination and their imagination.

Baby-led play and interaction

There is no need to formally 'teach' a baby. Your baby is learning all the time through sight, sound, smell, touch and taste. Joining in activities with your baby and taking cues from them is the best way to guide them through their enormous learning curve. Try things out and see how they respond.

Cause and effect

Remember, when they persist in throwing their toys out of the pram or hurling their porridge on the floor, they are actually learning about cause and effect – 'If I do A, then B happens' – and the laws of gravity. Call it a science lesson!

'I feel so strongly that it is important to respect the child's natural curiosity, inquisitiveness and autonomy, and offer a healthy use of language or model of behaviour for unwanted/ dangerous behaviour (for example, I say "yucky" or "hurt baby" instead of "no" etc).'

Avvai, mum to two children (aged one and four).

Everyday toys

Babies don't need expensive toys to play. They are just as happy playing with everyday items that they see you handling around the house. Banging things with wooden spoons and filling plastic containers with things can be old favourites! Make sure that you don't give your baby small items that they could choke on.

Words

Talking together

Babies love being talked to. Even though your baby doesn't understand what you are saying, they will enjoy your attention and interaction. If you chat away to your baby, they will smile and make noises back. They are never too young to start having a conversation.

Reading together

As well as being talked to, babies also love being read to. You can buy soft fabric books that your baby can hold and chew, as well as brightly coloured board books, which your baby can handle without tearing.

Babies soon find favourite books and enjoy hearing the same story over and over again as they learn to anticipate what comes next and even join in! Helping your child to develop a love of books and reading early in life is a wonderful gift.

Out and about

Getting out and about is an important part of expanding baby's play opportunities and development. It doesn't have to be anything overly adventurous. Even a trip to the local park will be exciting for your baby with all the new sights, sounds and smells to take in.

'Leila's favourite thing is books, and she'll happily sit on my knee and make me read through every book on her bookshelf. She loves textured books and lift the flap books, and she's just started to like "Peepo" and shouts "babo!"'

Dawn, mum to Leila (aged 10 months).

To alleviate any potential stress for yourself, make sure you are well prepared when you go out with a stocked changing bag and any feeding equipment you might need. As tempting as it might seem to pop to the shops 'freestyle', you may well regret leaving that muslin cloth and spare Babygro at home twenty minutes later when your baby pukes everywhere! It is amazing how much stuff one can need for a quick trip to the shops!

'Play is mostly unstructured and depends on what we feel like or if I need to get out and get fresh air and adult company. Sometimes it's just rolling around on the bed and jumping in muddy puddles or climbing slides.'

Avvai, mum to two children (aged one and four).

Summing Up

Pre-verbal babies have a range of ways of communicating, such as through crying, babbling, eye contact, facial expressions and body language. Take cues from your baby when pacing your interaction and play together.

Your baby is learning all the time through everyday experiences. There is no need to buy expensive toys, as household objects will be of immense interest to your baby. Talking and reading to your baby is a great way of helping them to develop their early language skills.

Chapter Nine

Weaning

'I could barely contain myself as I held out the plastic spoon. Smallboy stared at it, his mouth open and eyes glittering. He mulched it about in his mouth for a few seconds and swallowed it. In went another spoonful.' Extract from the author's journal, written in the first year of motherhood.

Weaning your baby on to solid food is an exciting milestone for any parent. Watching your baby react to different tastes and textures provides hours of amusement. It's just as well, because cleaning the splattered food off the floor and walls provides hours of work too!

When to start

Current Department of Health guidelines recommend starting to wean your baby on to solids at six months (after exclusive breastfeeding for the first six months). However, there is no magic date and it is generally best to be led by your baby's readiness. Some 'hungry babies' do well with weaning before the six-month mark. Others are not at all interested at six months. Health visitors will tell you not to start before 17 weeks because a baby's kidneys are not sufficiently developed.

Signs of readiness

Your baby will usually let you know when they are ready! Signs of readiness include:

- Being able to sit upright unaided.
- No longer appearing full after their usual feed, wanting another feed soon after.

'Come his six-month birthday, I sat him in his highchair, tied a bib around his neck and offered that first spoonful of pureed apple – expecting him to wolf it down eagerly as all his little friends had done. But he just wasn't interested. He clamped his lips shut and turned his face away.'

Fiona, mum to Eric (aged 14 months).

- Showing an interest in what you are eating, possibly trying to grab food and put it in their mouth.

Your baby does not need to have teeth to start weaning. They can chew soft foods with their gums.

What you will need

You don't really need much in the way of special equipment to start weaning your baby. However, if you walk into the baby section of your local department store, you may be mistaken into thinking otherwise.

Packets of baby rice and other specially designed baby food, non-slip feeding bowls, spoons, plastic bibs, baby recipe books, weaning cubes, high chairs, booster seats, splash mats and even special baby food processors are available.

Your usual kitchen equipment will cater for most tasks. You can boil or steam vegetables with whatever you normally use to cook your own food. A standard hand blender or food processor will create purees, and a fork or potato masher is fine for achieving lumpier textures. Ice cube trays are useful for freezing small portions of puree. In fact, the only thing you really need is a decent high chair.

Choosing a high chair

There are many different high chairs on the market, from your basic cheap and cheerful plastic numbers to stylish multi-function wooden designer products which convert to standalone chairs, or table and chairs for toddlers. Some have removable trays, which helps with cleaning and are useful for later on, when you might want to seat your baby directly at the table in their chair.

As long as your baby is comfortable and secure, the rest is immaterial. If it is important to you that the chair matches your dining room furniture, you won't be disappointed with the range on the market, although you might faint at the price tag of some of the elite models!

As an alternative to a high chair, you can also buy soft padded booster seats and cloth contraptions that fit over an existing dining room chair. These are generally cheaper, easily transportable and take up less room, so ideal if space is at a premium. Some of the plastic booster seats even include a tray.

Introducing first foods

There are two main approaches to weaning:

- Spoon-led weaning – where you begin by spooning pureed food directly into your baby's mouth and move on to mashed food etc.
- Baby-led weaning – where you put baby-sized food directly in front of your baby and let them feed themselves with supervision.

It is possible to combine both methods, for example, feeding your baby pureed vegetables from a spoon and giving them some bread to hold and feed themselves with.

Even if you are spoon-feeding, you still need to be led by your baby. If they turn away or push the food away, they are telling you that they don't want to eat. Never force a baby to eat.

With either method, it's important to never leave your baby unattended while feeding, to prevent choking.

Spoon-led weaning

The traditional pattern for spoon-led weaning is to start with baby rice, followed by pureed vegetables once your baby has 'mastered' rice and then move on to pureed fruit, before introducing other textures.

Your health visitor might advise working through a gradual programme, such as baby rice once a day to start for a week before assessing how your baby is getting on. Again, there are no hard and fast rules, and if you prefer to be led by your baby, don't worry too much about sticking to a programme. Babies eat when they are hungry, and refuse food when they are full and if they are unsure about the taste or texture or are experiencing any digestive discomfort.

'I did baby-led weaning with both my children. The first time, I didn't know that was what it was called – my eldest just refused to eat pureed food and wanted to eat what we were eating, the same with my second child.'

Avvai, mum to two children (aged one and four).

Combining with milk feeds

Of course, your baby will still be taking milk feeds when they start weaning. As they get used to solids, they will naturally take less milk. Initially, offer your baby their usual milk feeds.

Traditionally, spoon-led weaning involves beginning with one or two teaspoons of food per day, often at the time of their second feed. You then move on to offering solids with the third feed as well, and work up to offering solids for breakfast, lunch and tea, with morning and afternoon snacks.

Baby rice

Baby rice can be purchased in supermarkets and most baby departments. It looks like a packet of powder that you reconstitute. Always follow the instructions on the packet and temperature-taste the food before offering to your baby.

Baby rice is probably the blandest of foods that you could get. If you've tasted it, you'll understand what I'm saying. It has practically zero flavour! Starting with something this neutral means it won't be a shock to your baby's delicate taste buds.

Purees

Health visitors generally advise offering pureed vegetables before fruit, the theory being that if you introduce fruit first, they might develop a sweet tooth. There are many different vegetables that you can start with. Sweeter vegetables such as broccoli, sweet potato, carrots, parsnips and butternut squash are often favourites. Babies are programmed not to like bitter foods. You can mix breast milk or formula milk into the puree to begin with.

If you cook batches of fruit and vegetables in bulk, you can freeze portions to defrost later on for your baby, so you don't have to cook every time they eat. Of course, you can also buy ready-made baby food and puree, but this does work out to be more expensive. If you are out and about, an avocado or banana is very easy to mash instantly for a natural 'ready meal' on the go!

Be adventurous

Initially, you might want to offer one food at a time and then move on to mixing flavours together e.g. parsnip and broccoli etc. Once your baby is happily eating baby rice, pureed fruit and vegetables, it's a good idea to get more adventurous and vary their diet so they don't get too stuck in their ways, expecting the same old food all the time!

Babies can eat pureed or mashed versions of what you eat. Just make sure that you don't add salt to theirs.

Textures

The traditional spoon-led weaning approach usually presumes that baby gets used to pureed food before moving on to mashed food and introducing other textures, such as lumpy food. Food gradually becomes more recognisable until eventually, they are eating 'normal' food!

Cereals are an ideal introduction to lumpy textured food. You can buy specially designed baby cereals or just offer your baby a soft cereal such as porridge or Weetabix mixed with breast milk or formula. You can also try adding yoghurt and fruit to vary the taste and texture.

Easy first 'real meals' that are popular with babies include:

- Macaroni cheese with mixed vegetables.
- Vegetable risotto.
- Mashed jacket potato with baked beans.
- Spaghetti Bolognese or carbonara (meat or vegetarian).
- Tomato soup.

Finger foods

Babies love feeding themselves finger foods. Ideal finger foods include:

- Pieces of fruit – seedless grapes and slices of soft fruits such as peach, pear and banana are ideal to start with.

- Hand-sized pieces of steamed vegetables – such as broccoli and cauliflower.
- Raw vegetables – such as carrots and cucumber can also be offered, although your child may suck and chew on them rather than actually eat them at first.
- Bread sticks – ideal with pureed dips.
- Rice cakes – you can buy the baby-sized variety and add different toppings.

Baby-led weaning

Advocates of baby-led weaning don't believe it is necessary to go through the rigmarole of pureeing everything you put in your baby's mouth when you start weaning. According to the baby-led approach, you can just put baby-sized versions of the family meal in front of your baby at mealtimes and let them feed themselves with supervision.

Drinks

At the start of weaning, milk (breast or formula) will provide most of your baby's nutrients and make up most of their daily calories. The balance will gradually shift so that your baby will get most of their nutrients and calories from their food, although milk can remain a supplement for the whole of the first year and beyond.

As soon as your baby starts regularly eating solids, they will need to drink water as well as milk. You can also offer diluted unsweetened fruit juice at mealtimes.

If you have been breastfeeding up to this stage, there is no need to introduce a bottle. Your baby can go straight to drinking from a beaker or cup. Likewise, bottle-fed babies can be introduced to a beaker or cup at around six months. At first you can hold the beaker or cup for your baby, but they will soon want to have a go at holding it themselves!

'My advice would be: don't worry about the six-month date - your baby will take to solids when they are ready. Also, the "approved" baby foods - baby rice, bland purees - may just not be exciting enough to tempt your baby away from the beloved milk.'

Fiona, mum to Eric (aged 14 months).

Case study

Fiona's son, Eric, was showing none of the signs of being interested in solids as he approached six months. Nevertheless, as all the information about weaning given by the NHS stressed the importance of starting solids by then, beginning with one teaspoon of baby rice, Fiona started the weaning process.

Fiona says her son just wasn't interested and would clamp his lips shut when she tried to put a spoon near his mouth. By seven months, nothing had changed. He loved his milk and he didn't want anything else. By eight months, Eric was just as uninterested in puree, but now starting to pick up bits of pasta and broccoli and occasionally taking tiny nibbles. By nine months, he would eat the odd baby biscuit, but was still totally uninterested in puree and still screaming whenever the spoon came anywhere near his mouth.

Meanwhile, the health visitors kept insisting that breast milk was not sufficient for a baby after six months and Fiona began to get very anxious, imagining that her son would still be breastfeeding when he started school! By ten months, Eric had started picking up little bits of whatever the rest of the family were eating – beef stew, potatoes, carrots, pasta. Sometimes, Fiona would put food in his mouth on her finger and one morning she felt a sharp little point – his first tooth! Over the next month, four more teeth burst through and his eating increased dramatically.

'Leila became really interested in our food at four and a half months, so I started giving her slices of apple to hold and suck on. At six months we started to give her nectarines and vegetables. She would hold a whole nectarine and bury her face in it, and then cry if she dropped it.'

Dawn, mum to Leila (aged 10 months).

Summing Up

Government guidelines recommend starting to wean your baby on to solids around the six-month mark. However, it is important to be led by your baby – they will show you when they are ready!

There are two main approaches to weaning – spoon-led weaning and baby-led weaning. It is possible to combine the two approaches by offering traditional first baby foods, such as puree on a spoon, as well as finger food.

'If only the health visitors had said to me, "Don't worry, your baby will start eating solids when he's ready" then I wouldn't have wasted so much time fretting – as, of course, that is exactly what happened.'

Fiona, mum to Eric (aged 14 months).

Chapter Ten

Looking After Yourself

'Picture the scene. You're kicking back on a sunlounger, drink of choice in one hand, fave novel in the other, the sun beating down on you. Suddenly, a huge wave sweeps over you, washing the pina colada and Jodi Picoult away, and dragging you against the rocks.' Extract from the author's journal, written in the first year of motherhood.

Let's face it, looking after a baby is hard work and when you become a parent, life changes beyond recognition. The early days can be something of a shock. No matter how prepared you thought you were for a baby to enter your life, you never really know how your life will change and how you will feel until you are in the midst of your new life, sleepless nights, chaos and all!

When you have a baby, it can be hard to find the time to look after yourself. To suddenly have another person dependent on you for all their needs can be overwhelming and your own needs can often be overlooked. However, it is vital that you are looked after and that your own needs are catered for. This is easier said than done with a little person in tow, but with a little organising and negotiation it is just about possible.

The five As

The five golden As for looking after yourself are:

- *Allow* yourself to let everything slip, apart from caring for your baby and yourself. Now is not the time to be chastising yourself for slovenly housekeeping. Allow yourself the time to just be and to bond with baby. Go with the flow, focusing on your baby's needs and your own needs.

- *Ask* for help! People cannot read your mind. There is absolutely no point in being too proud to ask if you'd like someone to do something for you. Now is not the time for thinking, 'If they really cared, they would offer help/just do it without needing to be asked!' Sometimes, people are afraid of butting in, in case their help is seen as interference.

- *Accept* all offers of help, whether it's an offer to bring you some groceries, take the baby for an hour or come and cook you a meal. If you say no, they might not ask again! If you are starting to feel bombarded by visitors and just can't face another well-meaning 'helper', be honest and explain that you really appreciate their offer but are a bit tired to see anyone today. Would they like to come round tomorrow/next week?

- *Actively* encourage your partner (if you have one) to get as involved as possible with the baby. If you are breastfeeding, your partner can still wind the baby and change their nappy in the night. Don't fuss if your partner doesn't do it your way. As the saying goes, 'Don't sweat the small stuff'. If you keep telling your partner that they aren't doing things right, they may feel scared to try, or get resentful.

- *Appreciate* those who help you, whether it's your partner, your mother-in-law or the next-door neighbour. You might be thinking, 'I should jolly well think they should be helping me!' but remember that 'thank you' goes a long way.

> 'I have found that mums generally put a brave face on things. As we get chatting, things come out that people might not want to admit to a bunch of strangers, and gradually the group opens up.'
>
> Pauline, mum to two children (aged one and three).

Postnatal check-up

New mothers will be invited for a postnatal check-up, normally by their GP. Often, the baby's six-week check is arranged at the same time. This can be a good opportunity to ask any questions that you may have post-birth, so you might like to write a list of questions before your check-up.

The check-up should cover the physical, psychological and social aspects of having a new baby. This will include discussing any worries about how your body is healing, your health post-birth, how you are feeling emotionally, any worries you have about the baby and what social support you have. There will also be the opportunity to discuss breastfeeding.

If you feel that you need any particular type of support, you can ask your GP for a referral.

Examination

Your doctor may feel ('palpate') your abdomen to determine whether your womb has returned to its normal position. They will also probably check your blood pressure. A vaginal examination may be performed if you had stitches or if you are having any problems that need investigating.

Getting back into shape

Although we are confronted by images in the media of celebrities pinging back into their size six skinny jeans two weeks after giving birth, alas, for most new mothers this isn't the norm. It takes nine months for a woman's body to grow a baby and many say it takes another nine months for the body to return to 'normal'.

It can take a little bit of time to come to terms with your post-baby body but your belly will not resemble a collapsed soufflé for long! Of course, pregnancy and childbirth do change the body in various ways and not everything will necessarily go back to how it was. Yes, your body may be different than it was before but remember that bodies are beautiful in all shapes and sizes, and yours has performed an amazing feat!

Breastfeeding

Breastfeeding can help you to shift the baby bulge a bit quicker. Also, be aware that saggy boobs are actually caused by hormonal changes in pregnancy rather than by breastfeeding so don't let that put you off!

'Get time to yourself. Do the dreaded pelvic floor exercises. Exercise, whether it is walking, swimming or the gym. Whatever it is you will feel better afterwards. Meet your friends without the baby!'

Caroline, mum to Aimee (aged four months).

Relationships

Your partner

It is inevitable that relationships go through changes once you become a parent. If you have spent a long time together with your partner as a couple, it can come as something of a shock to now have three people in the relationship!

Just as you are learning to relate to your new baby and settle into your new role as a parent, you will also be learning how to relate to your partner in their new role as Mummy or Daddy.

However much you discussed parenting issues before baby came along, the chances are there will be certain areas where you will both have wildly differing views on how things should be done! Try to keep an open mind, keep calm and never underestimate the importance of compromise!

Sharing tasks

If you are raising a child as part of a couple, it is important that you share parenting tasks.

Sex and intimacy

It's that tricky question that people often skirt around after childbirth: 'When should we be having sex again?' Of course, the answer is when you both want to. It is generally considered safe to have sexual intercourse at around six weeks after childbirth, provided there are no complications. Many women like to wait until their postnatal check-up and discuss any potential concerns with the doctor, to be on the safe side.

Sex may be the last thing on your mind when you haven't slept for a month and your boobs are sore. Even if you do both feel ready, the opportunities for one-on-one time can be limited in the early weeks and months!

It can be strange to have sex for the first time after childbirth and it is natural for both partners to feel a little nervous. Talk to one another about your feelings and any worries, and take things slowly. If you aren't ready for full sexual intercourse, remember that there are other ways of being intimate.

The most important thing is to make sure that you show your partner how much you love them and that you still find them attractive, even if things aren't progressing in the bedroom!

Interesting fact

Remember that you can conceive again very soon after childbirth, so remember to use contraception when you do resume your sex life!

Friends and family

You might also find that your relationship with your own parents changes once you have a child and empathise with what they went through in raising you! Similarly, your relationships with other family members and friends, with or without children, may go through changes as your life and focus will have altered.

Maternity leave

There are two types of statutory maternity leave in the UK: ordinary maternity leave and additional maternity leave. At the time of publication, all working women who become pregnant are entitled to nine months' ordinary maternity leave (claiming Statutory Maternity Pay or Maternity Allowance). You may also be entitled to additional unpaid leave, depending on your employment situation.

Government policy in this area is subject to change. You can find up-to-date information on maternity rights from Maternity Action or your local Citizens Advice Bureau (see the help list for details).

Returning to work

Although you may have given a lot of consideration to whether or when to return to work after having your baby, it can be difficult to predict how you will feel when the time comes. Your decisions will be based on many factors, emotional and practical.

Some women plan to return to work quite soon after having a baby and then decide that they are unable to leave the baby and extend their maternity leave period. Others may plan to have a longer time off and then find they miss working life and want to return to work sooner.

For further information on finding a work/life balance and on your rights when returning to work, you may wish to read the Need2Know publication *Working Mothers: The Essential Guide (*Denise Tyler, Need2Know*)*.

Seeking support

Looking after a new baby is undeniably hard work. We all have times when we feel at sea and need a little help. It is important to remember that seeking help and support is not a sign of weakness. Rather, it shows that you are being sensible and proactive in working towards overcoming challenges.

Bumps and babies groups

A popular support network for new parents is the 'bumps and babies group'. These groups may be run by charities such as NCT (National Childbirth Trust) or the local council via a children's centre or similar.

A bumps and babies group gives new mums (and some are open to dads too) the opportunity to meet other new parents in their local area. They are usually open to pregnant women towards the end of their pregnancy and to parents of young babies. Getting together with other parents who may be going through similar challenges to you can be very helpful.

Case study

Pauline, mum to two children (aged one and three) had a horrible time with the birth of her first daughter, to the extent that it almost put her off having more children. In order to deal with the experience of giving birth a second time, she had counselling to explore the issues surrounding the first birth, which she found invaluable in letting go of guilt and moving on.

Pauline decided that, since she had so much help from other mums in getting over her experience, she would try to give something back by getting involved in her local branch of NCT (National Childbirth Trust). Pauline volunteers as a New Parent Support Coordinator, a role which she shares with a friend.

They organise nights out in the pub (!) where bumps and their partners can meet and chat before they have their babies. This is followed up with two organised meetings for each group, normally hosted at Pauline's house. The tea groups are a good opportunity for mums to get to know each other, chat about their birth and small baby experiences, and then continue to meet as their babies grow.

Your health visitor

All families with children under five have a named health visitor. A health visitor helps families to stay healthy. They can offer advice on a range of matters, including feeding, sleeping, growth and development.

You can find their contact details in your 'little red book', which would have been issued to you soon after your baby was born. Or contact your local health centre or children's centre. They may offer drop-in sessions or appointment-only services.

Do what is right for you

Whether consulting a health professional or reading an advice guide, it is important to remember that the views of experts are not the words of God. There are usually a range of different schools of thought relating to any one issue. It is up to you to decide what parenting ideas and approaches work best for you and your family. It is okay to question 'the experts'!

Social norms and parenting practices vary according to culture and social context. For example, in some cultures, it is normal to co-sleep with babies, toddlers and older children, whereas in Western society, this is often frowned upon.

Trust yourself. If something feels wrong to you, according to your own personal values, beliefs and world view, then don't do it. Conversely, if you discover an approach that feels right for your family, follow your instincts. You don't have to do what everyone else is doing!

What I have tried to do in this book is to present you with information, options and ideas. What you decide to do with this is entirely up to you. I would encourage you to question everything!

Summing Up

Looking after a baby brings lots of joy but is undeniably hard work. It is important to be able to ask for help at times. Meeting other new parents and developing a support network can be invaluable.

Remember that it is okay to question 'the experts'. It is up to you to decide what parenting ideas and approaches work best for you and your family.

I hope this book has proved to be a useful guide and has given you some ideas and inspiration to help you as you adjust to life as a parent.

Need2Know

Help List

Association of Breastfeeding Mothers

Telephone: 08444 122 949 (helpline)
Email: counselling@abm.me.uk
Website: www.abm.me.uk
UK charity founded by mothers for mothers, to provide information and support around breastfeeding.

Association for Postnatal Illness

Telephone: 020 7386 0868
Website: www.apni.org
Provides information and support to mothers and fathers with postnatal illness/depression.

The Breastfeeding Network

National Breastfeeding Helpline: 0300 100 0212
Bengali/Sylheti Supporterline: 0300 456 2421
Website: www.breastfeedingnetwork.org.uk
Provides information and support on breastfeeding.

Citizens Advice Bureau

Telephone for details of your local bureau.
Offers free, confidential, independent advice on a range of matters including benefits, housing and employment rights.
UK advice website: www.adviceguide.org.uk

Citizens Advice England and Wales

Telephone: 020 7833 2182
Website: www.citizensadvice.org.uk

Citizens Advice Northern Ireland

Telephone: 028 9023 1120
Website: www.citizensadvice.co.uk

Citizens Advice Scotland

Telephone: 0131 550 100
Website: www.cas.org.uk

Contact a Family

Telephone: 0800 808 3555
Textphone: 0800 808 3556
Email: helpline@cafamily.org.uk
Website: www.cafamily.org.uk
UK charity providing support, advice and information for families with disabled children.

Directgov Family Information Directory

Website: http://childcarefinder.direct.gov.uk
England public services website including a search facility for childcare providers.

Disability, Pregnancy and Parenthood International (DPPI)

Telephone: 0800 018 4730
Textphone: 0800 018 9949
Email: info@dppi.org.uk
Website: www.dppi.org.uk
UK information charity for disabled parents, and the publisher of the international journal on disabled parenting, Disability, Pregnancy & Parenthood international.

Emma's Diary

Website: www.emmasdiary.co.uk
A privately run company offering online information and forums relating to pregnancy and new parenthood. The editorial content of Emma's Diary is published in association with the Royal College of General Practitioners.

Foundation for the Study of Infant Deaths

Telephone: 0808 802 6868 (helpline)
Website: www.fsid.org.uk
Helpline offers support and advice on prevention of cot death, as well as services for bereaved parents.

Home-Start

Telephone: 0800 068 6368
Email: info@home-start.org.uk
Website: www.home-start.org.uk
National charity with local schemes of volunteers throughout the UK offering support and practical help to parents with children under the age of five years.

Maternity Action

Telephone: 020 7253 2288
Website: www.maternityaction.org.uk
UK charity offering advice and information on maternity rights.

The Nappy Site

Website: www.thenappysite.co.uk
Second-hand nappy and baby care resources.

Netmums

Website: www.netmums.com
A network of local parenting websites offering online forums, coffee shops and professional guidance on parenting issues.

NCT (National Childbirth Trust)

Telephone: 0300 3300770
Breastfeeding line: 0300 3300771
Website: www.nct.org.uk
UK charity for parents offering information on pregnancy, birth and early parenthood. Also offers antenatal and postnatal classes and support.

NI Direct Government Services

Website: www.nidirect.gov.uk/index/parents/childcare/choosing-childcare
Northern Ireland public services website including a search facility for childcare providers.

Parentline Plus

Telephone: 0808 800 2222
Textphone: 0800 783 6783
Email: via website only
Website: www.parentlineplus.org.uk
A national charity offering help and support for parents through an innovative range of free, flexible, responsive services.

Scottish Childcare

Website: www.scottishchildcare.gov.uk
One stop shop for childcare information in Scotland.

Welsh Assembly Family Information Services

Website: http://wales.gov.uk/topics/childrenyoungpeople/parenting/familyinformationservices/
Welsh public services website including a search facility for childcare providers.

Book List

A Life's Work: On Becoming a Mother
By Rachel Cusk, Fourth Estate, London, 2001.

A Secure Base: Parent-Child Attachment and Healthy Human Development
by John Bowlby, Routledge (Tavistock professional book), London, 1988.

Dr. Spock's Baby and Childcare
By Benjamin Spock, Simon & Schuster, London, 2005 [1946].

Fatherhood – The Essential Guide
By Tim Atkinson, Need2Know, Peterborough, 2011.

Freeing Ourselves From The Mad Myths of Parenthood!
By Susan Jeffers, Hodder and Stoughton, London, 2005.

The Idle Parent
By Tom Hodgkinson, Hamish Hamilton, London, 2009.

Making Babies
By Anne Enwright, Vintage, London, 2005.

Misconceptions
By Naomi Wolff, Vintage, London, 2002.

New Babycare Book: A Practical Guide to the First Three Years
By Miriam Stoppard, Dorling Kindersley, London, 2002.

Of Woman Born, Motherhood as Experience and Institution
By Adrienne Riech, Norton, New York, 1986.

Postnatal Depression – The Essential Guide
By Catherine Burrows, Need2Know, Peterborough, 2010.

Working Mothers – The Essential Guide
By Denise Tyler, Need2Know, Peterborough, Updated version 2011.

References

Attachment Parenting International, www.attachmentparenting.org, accessed 6 April 2010.

Clinical Knowledge Summaries (CKS), 2009, *Postnatal depression* [online], www.cks.nhs.uk, accessed 8 January 2010.

Department of Health, *Statistical release: breastfeeding initiation and prevalence at 6-8 weeks*, www.dh.gov.uk/en/Publicationsandstatistics/ Publications/PublicationsStatistics/DH_116060, accessed 20 January 2011.

Environment Agency and Department for Environment, Food and Rural Affairs (DEFRA), *An updated lifecycle assessment study for disposable and reusable nappies*, Environment Agency, Bristol, 2008. http://randd.defra.gov.uk/Document. aspx?Document=WR0705_7589_FRP.pdf, accessed 27 January 2011.

Equality Act 2010. The Stationery Office Limited, London, 2010, www. legislation.gov.uk/uksi/2010/2317/pdfs/uksi_20102317_en.pdf, accessed 27 January 2011.

KGB answers, www.kgbanswers.com/on-average-how-many-diapers-does-a-baby-need-in-the-first-year/10985557, accessed 27 January 2011.

National Health Service, *NHS breastfeeding website* [online] www. breastfeeding.nhs.uk, accessed 26 March 2009.

National Health Service, NHS Choices, *Cot death: how to reduce the risk* [online] http://www.nhs.uk/livewell/childhealth0-1/pages/cotdeath.aspx, accessed 30 May 2011.

NCT (National Childbirth Trust), *Secure and insecure attachment,* NCT Information Centre [online], www.nct.org.uk/info-centre/information/view-66, accessed 5 November 2010.

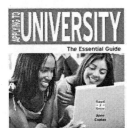
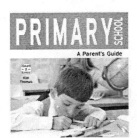
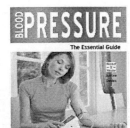
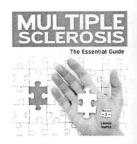